Man of the Woods

(Photo by Stephen S. Slaughter)

HERBERT F. KEITH, 1970

Man of the Woods

HERBERT F. KEITH

With Introduction and Notes by
PAUL F. JAMIESON

 SYRACUSE UNIVERSITY PRESS / THE ADIRONDACK MUSEUM
1972

Copyright © 1972 by Syracuse University Press, Syracuse, New York

ALL RIGHTS RESERVED

FIRST PAPERBACK PRINTING 1976

Library of Congress Cataloging in Publication Data

Keith, Herbert F
  Man of the woods.

     1. Adirondack Mountains—Social life and customs.
  I. Title.
  F127.A2K4   917.47'53   78-38507
  ISBN 0-8156-0126-3

IN MEMORY OF THE OSWEGATCHIE RIVER GUIDES I KNEW

BERT DOBSON	WALTER GATES
ART LEARY	JACK LOUDEN
BILL (W. J.) MacALEESE	JOHN McBROOM
LOREN MOORE	WILFRED MORRISON
CLARENCE PHILLIPS	GEORGE PRESTON
UNCLE STEVE WARD	JIM WELCH
JOHN OLSON	

INTRODUCTION

Herbert Keith lives between two worlds and is at home in both. His is the last mowed lawn at the edge of the village. South of the iron stakes that mark his property line are twenty-one air miles of unbroken Adirondack forest preserve, all the way past the headwaters of the Oswegatchie and the Beaver Stillwater to Big Moose.

Herb must have known what he was doing. Three times he had a choice between Wanakena and the more developed world outside, and three times—after high school in New York City, after service in World War I, and finally after a long tour of service in Europe in World War II—he chose Wanakena, the village in the forest. Each time the choice was deliberate, meaningful, and risky. It wasn't easy to make a living in Wanakena after the lumbering stopped. The third time was the riskiest of all. While abroad, Herb met and married a Bulgarian art student who spoke five languages and who had lived only in Sofia, Rome, and New York before Herb brought her to Wanakena in 1948. Results have justified the risk. The Keiths have raised a son and a daughter to maturity in the little Adirondack village. Mrs. Mimi Keith is a leading cultural influence there, painting in oils and giving art and music lessons. Not long ago she made a visit to Boston. She liked the art there, but that was all she liked. Nothing suits her now but her home at the edge of the woods. She even likes Adirondack winters.

Herb built the house himself with the many skills that an Adirondack native accumulates in order to survive. Long and low, it fits snugly into an angle of woods on south and west. It faces east across the mowed lawn to a bank of fireweed and, beyond that, to the old millpond, now a sanctuary for water-loving birds. On the north side only is there a hint of Herb's continuing contact with the developed world. It is a cement block building with an array of antennas, where until 1969 he ran a radio and TV maintenance shop and where he still goes in the mornings to talk with other ham radio operators.

It is never dull around Herb's place. People and animals come and go at all hours. Birds, squirrels, deer mice, and chipmunks come from the woods for a change of diet at his feeders. A curious doe or spotted fawn steps tentatively onto his lawn from the wall of trees. A black bear, having cleaned up the wild raspberries, prowls around his house looking for more sweets. A family of coons ambles in at dusk for supper. Mother coon has struck up an acquaintance with the house cat. After both have finished supper, they take a stroll together across the lawn, the little coons tagging behind, and say goodnight at the edge of the woods.

I knew Herb's house before I knew Herb himself. The thing that draws us wayfarers from the north across his property is the trail to High Falls, Five Ponds, and other points in the great South Woods. If we can hold out for the first six or seven miles through second-growth timber, we enter a primitive forest where no logging has ever taken place. Where Keith Drive ends at the iron stakes on Herb's south line, this trail begins.

We are a mixed lot, but we have two things in common—ambitious plans and, according to Herb, unfitness to carry them out. (Read his eighteenth chapter for a frank opinion of modern sportsmen.) Some of us turn back before reaching High Falls, and many more before achieving Pine Ridge, Nicks Pond, Five Ponds, Wolf Pond, and, through virgin spruce and hardwoods, remote and lonely Sand Lake. Herb sees us coming in and going out. The going-out spectacle usually confirms his suspicions at the going in. Sitting at his dining room table and looking out the window toward the staging area, I have shared both of these spectacles with him and know his reaction. When hikers arrive from the north, having crossed the one-lane auto bridge over the rapids of the Oswegatchie, they are careless in the sun. Herb doesn't share their confidence. He takes a quick inventory. Sneakers. Bare legs. Bare arms. An uncovered bald head. A pack that rides too low. Paper sacks to carry by hand. A bedroll tucked under arm or balanced on shoulder. Duffle dangling from a pole supported by the shoulders of two hikers of military bearing.

Hours or days later the same parties come out of the woods, slouched, straggling, scratching bites, limping to favor a blister inside a wet sneaker, glassy eyed, a little grim. What they need, says Herb, is an old-time Adirondack guide.

A few do-it-yourself sportsmen really know the woods and how to get along in them. To these Herb will open his heart. To the others he is still the perfect gentleman. It wasn't for nothing that he served apprenticeship to Wilfred Morrison, that ace of guides. He answers your questions patiently, including some you don't ask but should.

It is remarkable that Herbert Keith ever got around to writing a book at all. Year-round Adirondackers generally leave book writing to outsiders and summer residents. There is too much to do in the woods to waste time scribbling. Herbert Keith is that rarity, the native who has written a book about his life in the woods.

For nearly a century the Adirondack guide was the center of the literature of the region. He was celebrated as the true descendant of Leatherstocking and Boone. Even now, fifty years or more after the passing of the great guides (for a number of reasons, guiding persisted a little longer in the Oswegatchie-Cranberry country than in most other parts of the Adirondacks), you may run across a tribute to "the last of the Adirondack guides." But these profiles have a common limitation. They do not give the inside story. They are written by the party, not by the guide. Here is a book by an Adirondack guide speaking for himself and his fellows. The viewpoint is strikingly different.

Herbert Keith's book tells the story of the unique community of Wanakena, a lumber camp that grew into a village and a village that can no longer grow because it is surrounded by forest preserve; of the guides of the Oswegatchie River, Wilfred Morrison in particular; of the great green forest that has survived logging, fire, blowdown, and the use and abuse of sportsmen.

Of the author, his friend Wesley Hammond writes: "Herbert Keith is a quiet man who loves the great outdoors with all his heart. Some might say his formal education was meager, but his education in life and living is great. He lives a life of dignity and respect and restores one's belief in human nature." That is true of the man I too have come to know. But Herb is more complex than he first appears. It isn't only in space that he lives between two worlds, it is in time also. In one way, he is a modern, a technician. Engines and electronic gear excite him. He is skilled at operating and repairing them. But with another side of his nature he hates machines for upsetting the balance of the simpler and happier times he knew before the state highway reached the villages of Cranberry Lake and Wanakena in the late 1920s. There was something special about the area and its way of life in the closing years of the last century and the first thirty years of the present one. The people in the small villages, the lumber camps, and the summer cottages were so at harmony with their surroundings that they had the surplus energy to create a folklore. Herbert Keith was at home too in that world of feeling, human diversity, and humor—and still is.

PAUL F. JAMIESON, Editor of *The Adirondack Reader*

ACKNOWLEDGMENTS

I want to thank the following people for their generous assistance: Mr. and Mrs. Robert S. Lansing, Mrs. Pearl Morrison, Mrs. Marion Sawyer, Mrs. Cordelia Moyer, Mr. and Mrs. Keith Hamele, and Morris Coolidge, all of Wanakena; Mrs. Laura Ward, formerly of Wanakena, now of Saranac Lake; the late Mrs. Sam Spain, of Benson Mines; Mrs. Thelma Ritz, of Benson Mines; Fay Welch, of Erieville; Mr. and Mrs. Alfred S. Sheard, formerly of Cranberry Lake, now of Canton; Mrs. Josephine G. Mentley, of the St. Lawrence University Library, Canton; Mrs. Mary H. Biondi, St. Lawrence County historian, of Ogdensburg and Canton; A. T. Shorey, of Albany; Wesley Hammond, of Leicester; Edwin H. Ketchledge, professor of forest biology, of the State College of Forestry, Syracuse, and of the Cranberry Lake Biological Station; John B. Johnson, editor and publisher of the *Watertown Daily Times;* Dorothy A. Plum, of East Hill, Keene; and Barney Fowler. I wish also to thank those whose names appear under the photographs they contributed.

H. F. K.

Wanakena, N.Y.
June, 1971

CONTENTS

INTRODUCTION   vii

ACKNOWLEDGMENTS   xi

1. A Dream Come True   1

2. My Wonderland   4

3. Up the Oswegatchie
   With Wilfred   15

4. Camp Betsy   30

5. High Falls and Beyond   35

6. Forest Fires   46

7. The Big Fight   51

8. The General Store and
   the Hotel   56

9. Fishing and a Ride on
   the Mail Boat   63

10. Two Shames: Timber
    Thieves and a Motorboat
    at High Falls   72

11. Logging Ends, Ranger
    School Begins   81

12. About Hunting and
    Other Matters   88

13. Fun Up the River   96

14. Jim Welch   105

15. The Learys   109

16. A Captain, a Schoolteacher,
    an Old Wolf Hunter,
    and a Dog   116

17. A Guide's Hunting
    Camp   121

18. Sports and Engineers   127

19. High Life   139

20. Wilfred's Trial   145

21. The Oswegatchie
    Years Later   153

NOTES   157

MAPS:

Cranberry Lake Railroad and Logging Railroad of the Rich
   Lumber Company   5

The Oswegatchie and Cranberry Lake Region   95

Man of the Woods

1. A DREAM COME TRUE

"Hey fellows! Hey fellows! I'm going to the Adirondack Mountains. Oh boy! That's where Dr. Johnston and Lawyer Nichols shot the big buck last fall and Mr. Scott caught the big speckled trout." "Oh gee! Can't we go with you?" the fellows asked. The excitement of anticipation was to keep me awake two nights before it was time to leave. Those days of waiting seemed like weeks. My suitcase was crammed to the limit, and Mother packed three shoe boxes full of sandwiches and other food. From that day to this I have had the habit of traveling with more than enough. A summer visitor once asked a Wanakena guide if I had ever been to Sand Lake. The guide replied, "Hell no, he couldn't carry enough food to make that trip."

It was a beautiful June morning in 1907 when I got on the train and left my home in Ellicottville, New York, for the little village in the Adirondacks that I had heard so much about. It was thrilling to get off the train in Buffalo and board the New York Central bound for Syracuse. I had never traveled so fast in all my twelve years, and it seemed no time at all until the train stopped to let me off. In Syracuse I boarded the Watertown train. We waited for a long time before it started to move. It was an old train even then and surely lived up to its reputation of being slow. Fifty years later the same train was still running, but the slack in the old coach couplers had stretched so badly that it was said the last car arrived in Watertown five minutes later than the locomotive.

I had only one shoe box of food left when we crept into Watertown. I got off the train when I heard someone call, "All aboard for the C & A—Carthage, Harrisville, Benson Mines, and Newton Falls." I asked the conductor if the train went to Benson Mines, and when he said it did I climbed aboard. The New York Central had some famous old trains and still has a few, but it has never had one to compare with the old C & A (Carthage and Adirondack Branch) or Lumberjack and Gum Pickers

1

Special. Logging was the main job along the C & A. Picking spruce gum was a way of earning a little extra money. Agents from the gum makers came to the Adirondacks to buy up the gum pickers' harvest and send it to the factories to be processed and wrapped. Many people chewed it just as it came from the trees. The people who did nothing but gum picking for a living were the hippies of those days.

We were soon in motion. The first thing that happened before we got even to Carthage was that three beer kegs rolled out of the baggage car near Black River. A man wearing a red and black checkered wool shirt and with a peculiar smell jumped up and pulled a string two times. The train came to a screeching stop. The conductor came back and gave him the devil for causing the delay. The poor fellow tried to tell the conductor about the beer kegs, but the conductor ignored his explanation and told him again to leave the emergency cord alone. A middle-aged lady seated near me told me the man was a lumberjack and a stranger to the train line. She paused for some time and then said, "That was about the same place as the beer kegs roll out each trip." She laughed and added, "You will see plenty more of them fall off before you reach the end of the line."

I wanted to ask her what made the lumberjacks smell so funny and if they all smelled that way, but changed my mind and thought it would be better to ask some man. At Carthage several more lumberjacks got on board and in a few minutes we were again in motion. I was now seeing, hearing, smelling, and learning a lot about the typical Adirondack lumberjack. The odd smell was the thing I most wanted to find out about this new, to me, breed of man. With my nerve up I shyly asked a well-dressed man who sat ahead of me. He laughed long and heartily and finally replied, "Well, my boy, that perfume is nothing but a secret mixture of honest sweat, oil of tar, and citronella," and then went back to the paper he was reading.

I didn't dare ask any more questions at that time. I was still confused and wondering. The more I thought about it the more I knew I just had to find out about that perfume. So I decided to try and make friends with one of the lumberjacks and ask him for the answer I wanted so badly. I offered one of them a sandwich from my shoe box, which he quickly took and started to eat. As he chewed on my offering, he took a bottle out of his pocket and drank from it and then asked me, "Do you want a drink of tea?" I said yes and took a big swallow, for I was thirsty. In a second I was sure I had swallowed a lighted match or two. Choking and coughing, I quickly returned the bottle. The lumberjack

2

laughed. Without a doubt I had had my first taste of whiskey. He drank about half of the bottle and never quivered.

I decided that now was the time to ask my question concerning the perfume. So without further delay I asked, "Why do you lumberjacks use the perfume I smell?" He roared with laughter and asked me if I had ever heard of black flies, punkies, or speckle-winged gentlemen. I replied, "No, sir," and then he explained that I would see and feel plenty of them when I got in the woods. He said he had never before heard fly dope called perfume.

Soon we pulled into Harrisville, where the train crew unloaded the baggage and freight and then unloaded several of the lumberjacks who had passed out. I thought that the crew handled the freight more carefully than the men. We stopped next at Jayville, where we unloaded more freight, baggage, and lumberjacks.

When we arrived at Benson Mines, a large crowd of people was waiting for the evening train. Evidently this event was the high point of the day. Standing on the opposite side of the station house was the Cranberry Lake Railroad train, which consisted of a steam locomotive (Old Number 5) and two coaches. One of the coaches was a combination smoking car and baggage car. The Cranberry Lake train was waiting to take the passengers, express, mail, and baggage to Wanakena, its home terminal. As we loaded and started on the last six miles of my journey, we passed the Ellsworth Hotel, managed and owned by Sam Spain.

I thought it funny that the engine backed up pulling the coaches, but by asking questions again I learned this odd arrangement was necessary because there was no turntable at Benson Mines. About two miles from Wanakena we crossed over a high wooden trestle which allowed the train to sway from side to side. I was frightened, for it felt as if we were going to tip over. It wasn't long after this that the railroad people filled in the trestle with iron ore waste from Benson Mines so that the passengers and crew didn't have to hold their breath while crossing. Soon we passed a settlement called the French Camps after the French-Canadian lumberjacks who lived there. When we were about a mile from Wanakena, we went around a very sharp curve called Shannon's, where the wheel flanges squealed so loudly that one's ears rang. The people in Wanakena could hear this noise and used it as a signal to assemble at the depot for the evening excitement of watching the train come in and getting their mail.

My grandfather was there to meet me and told me Grandma had

3

END OF THE LINE, CRANBERRY LAKE RAILROAD
Train watchers eye arriving hotel guests on the boardwalk in front of the general store in Wanakena. The engine has backed from Benson Mines.
(Courtesy Genevieve Crocker)

stayed home in order to have a hot meal ready for me. This was good news, for I had eaten my last crumb from the shoe boxes several hours ago. I got up early the next morning and found that one of the neighbors had brought over some freshly caught speckled trout. I shall never forget my first breakfast of trout in the Adirondacks.

It is not clear how Wanakena got its name. Some old-timers say that it was named after an Indian maiden. Others say that Herbert Rich, one of the officials of the lumber company, saw the name on a Pullman car when they were on their way to purchase the property. They decided to use it for the lumber camp that was to turn into a village.

2. MY WONDERLAND

Shortly after 1900 the Rich Lumber Company exhausted their resources in Pennsylvania, came to this area, and purchased about sixteen thousand acres of virgin forest.[1] Their camp was located approximately in the center of this forest and of course later became known as Wanakena. The village is on the east or main branch of the Oswegatchie River

4

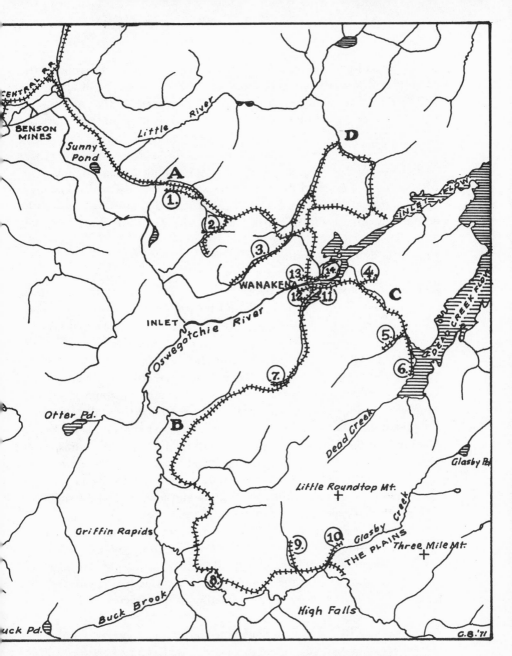

Cranberry Lake Railroad and Logging Railroads of the Rich Lumber Company. (Adapted by George Bowditch from a map by Robert S. Lansing)

KEY: (A) Main passenger line, Benson Mines to Wanakena, 6 miles. Chartered as the Cranberry Lake Railroad, it was used also in logging operations. (B) Logging railroad, Wanakena to the Plains, 9 miles. (C) Logging, Wanakena to Dead Creek Flow, 2½ miles. (D) Logging, the Crimmins Loop, 4 miles plus two short spurs. 1. Levenworth spur. 2. Flatrock spur. 3. French Camp spur. 4. McCarthy Creek siding. 5. Cucumber Creek spur. 6. Jack Works (on Dead Creek Flow). 7. Passing siding. 8. Jack Works (on river). 9. Carlson switch. 10. Boiling Spring spur. 11. Sawmill. 12. Other mills. 13. Car barn, scale house. 14. Depot and dock.

about five airline miles upstream from where this main feeder meets the old original part of Cranberry Lake. In 1867 a dam was built across the outlet of the lake to increase the water storage area so that, in times of drought, water could be let out to improve navigation and run the sawmills, paper mills, factories, and power plants on the lower river.

The dam increased the surface area of the lake from five to nearly eleven square miles by flooding the swales along feeder streams. The flooded areas are called flows, the largest being Dead Creek Flow. The upper Oswegatchie forms Inlet Flow, also called simply the Flow. Others are known as West, South, Chair Rock, East, and Brandy Brook flows. These tentacles, along with the main body of the lake, make up about 160 miles of shoreline.[2]

Thirty islands are important enough to have names. Others are just dimples of rock where gulls perch. Some are so low lying that the trees on them seem adrift. Pretty Birch and Buck islands are heavily wooded. Joe Indian, the largest, was cut off the mainland of the original lake by the rising water above the dam.

When I first came to the woods in 1907 and for several years after, most of the land around Cranberry Lake was still privately owned. Lumber camps, several hotels, and about one hundred summer cottages were scattered around the shore of the main lake. Nearly all of this development had taken place within the preceding ten or twelve years. There was still much uncut timber around the lake and much unspoiled wilderness. The people who managed and worked for the hotels, the guests who returned year after year, 'the summer residents in the cottages, and even many of the lumberjacks and jobbers loved Cranberry Lake as they did no other place on earth, and each loved it in his own way. There were many characters among them. Outstanding were those lovable woodsmen, the once famous, now all but forgotten Adirondack guides. Those fine men were my friends, and I want to tell about them and about what the country around Cranberry was like before the improved roads and the automobile spoiled most of its charm and tranquility.

Before the Rich Lumber Company moved in, there was only one building near the site of the new village of Wanakena. This was a little cabin on the southwest bank of Inlet Flow at the Narrows, over a mile below the rapids. The site is called Yale Point, and the cabin was built before 1901 by some Yale College professors who vacationed there. The professors never returned after the lumbering started. The main part of the cabin is still intact today, though it has been added to.

In 1902 the lumber company constructed a railroad from Benson Mines to the site which was to be their main operating point, and the little village of Wanakena was born. Houses in sections were brought in on the railroad from the previous lumbering operation in Pennsylvania, and of course many new places were also built. The new Hotel Wanakena and the Rich and Andrews General Store were the largest such places for miles around, so they soon built up an amazing business. A suspension footbridge was built across the river, and a little further upstream a railroad bridge was constructed to give access to the south side, where the large sawmills and log ponds were being located. Two miles from the village large springs of cold water were tapped, and water pipes were laid to bring the water into every house in town. (After the people had been enjoying this spring water for fifty years, the Albany Board of Health decided that it was unsafe to drink, so a chlorinator was installed. Now when you take a drink, you can think of how Albany saved your life.) Sewers were put in, electric light plants built, fire mains laid and prepared so as to avoid freezing in winter. In 1904 the village was one of a very few in the entire Adirondacks that could boast of such modern conveniences. In 1907 it had a population of nearly five hundred.

CABIN AT YALE POINT ON THE NARROWS
Built prior to 1901 by Yale College professors as a summer camp, this was the only building nearby when the Rich Lumber Company founded Wanakena. It is still standing, though remodeled.

(Courtesy Mr. and Mrs. Fred L. Keith)

A SIGHT NEVER TO BE SEEN AGAIN
A sleigh loaded with logs on an iced main haul road. Bulldozers, tractors, and trucks have taken over this work.

Lumberjacks came in from Canada to supplement the crews which had been brought in from Pennsylvania. The Canadians built a group of camps which, as mentioned before, were called the French Settlement. The employees that had worked for the company in Pennsylvania were mostly Swedes and Italians, and they built their own settlements.

The method of getting the logs out in Pennsylvania wouldn't work in this locale. It cost the Rich Lumber Company many extra dollars when they refused the offers made by experienced Adirondack jobbers to get the logs out for them. In Pennsylvania the logging was done by building slides down the steep mountainsides and then building railroads to haul the logs the rest of the way. Our mountains weren't steep enough for log slides. But in the Adirondacks there was snow enough, and it was cold enough, to build ice roads to haul the logs out on. The lumber company didn't approve of the use of such roads and proceeded to build expensive railroads into the woods. A glance at the Wanakena railroad map gives some idea of the unnecessary expense the company went to. The old-time logging jobbers of the area, with tears in their eyes, pleaded for contracts to bring out the logs on ice roads and by horse-drawn sleighs. Hundreds of dollars could have been saved by their skill and know-how.

8

But their pleas were ignored. As it turned out, these jobbers did play a very important role during the next ten years of lumbering.

While the mill was being constructed, the company built a railroad to within a mile of their southern boundary at the Herkimer County line. This railroad terminated at the Plains, nine miles from Wanakena and one mile from High Falls on the Oswegatchie River. Another branch of the railroad was built from the mill to Dead Creek Flow, a distance of two and a half miles. At the point where the railroad met Dead Creek Flow, a jack works was built. It consisted of a boom device, run by steam power, made to lift the logs out of the water and place them on the logging railroad cars. This was another expensive operation, for the logs could have been left on the sleighs which brought them to this location in the first place and hauled a few more miles to the mill. Another railroad branched off the main line one mile from the village and wandered around for about five miles on the northern boundary of the company property. Several additional short spurs helped to make up the logging railroad system.

Since the railroad was built over some fairly steep grades, it was necessary for the locomotives to be of the Shay geared type. These funny looking little locomotives used gears to drive the driving wheels instead of the conventional side rods. When one heard one of these engines coming down the track, it sounded as if it were traveling at least ninety miles per hour, but because of the gearing the speed was closer to ten

SHAY GEARED ENGINE OF THE RICH LUMBER COMPANY
Gears instead of side rods drove the wheels of the logging train engines. The engineer (center) is Eugene Madison.

miles per hour. The log cars were built with a bunk on each end which had a piece of light railroad rail spiked to it so that the logs could roll on and off easily.

When the millpond was finished, the exhaust from the steam engines used to run the mill was piped into the pond to prevent freezing in winter. The railroad was built along the edge of the pond and a rollway built so that the logs could be rolled off the cars into the pond. The railroad bed was slanted toward the pond to give the logs a good start as soon as the chains which held them were loosened. A lumberjack loosened the chains by hitting a special toggle with his peavey and then quickly jumping out of the way. This was a dangerous job. Only lively and clearheaded men were picked for it.

The millpond served several important purposes in the lumbering process, one of which was to allow easy sorting of the logs for each day's run. A chute from the top of the mill ran down into the water. When logs were led into the mouth of this chute with a long pikepole, the hooks of an endless chain bit into them and dragged them up into the mill. When the logs were being skidded on the skidding trails, they gathered considerable dirt and lots of small stones and grit. The pond was useful in helping to wash this dirt away. A spray of water was directed at the logs as they passed up the chute to further help in cleansing them.

Near the top of the mill was a little shanty in which a company scaler sat with his scaling stick and tally sheet. Each log was scaled and checked to the credit of the jobber whose mark was stamped on the end. It appeared that the company scaler's stick always measured less than the jobber's scale. Today the unions have this situation pretty much reversed.

The saws used in the mill were huge band saws. If you have never seen such a large band saw, you may think of a huge endless belt made of steel running upon two large flat-surfaced pulleys some eight feet or more in diameter. One of these pulleys was located in the lower part of the mill and the other above the floor on which the carriage ran carrying the logs to be sawed. The teeth on the edge of this so-called steel belt were bent alternately in opposite directions to give "set" so that the saw cut would be wider than the saw to prevent binding. If the saw did bind, it might break and whip around among the workers with disastrous results. Lumber mill workers were of course aware of this danger and tried to keep it from happening.

When the logs came up the chute from the millpond, they were rolled onto a platform to make room for the logs following. The carriage was mounted on wheels which ran on a track. One end of the carriage was fastened to a piston rod operating in and out of a steam cylinder. As the piston was operated, the carriage moved to and fro at the operator's will. The man operating the carriage was called the sawyer. Two men who rode on the carriage handled the log after it had been rolled off the platform onto the carriage. One of these men was called the setter. His job was to move the log toward the saw and adjust for thickness of board. The other man, called a dogger, operated the dogs that held the log in place while it was being sawed. The sawyer moved the carriage with the log attached up to the fast moving band saw. As the carriage continued to advance, the saw, with a whiz and hum, cut off the first board, which dropped onto rollers.

The board slid on these rollers to a set of gang saws, where the uneven bark edges were cut off. The waste was taken outside the mill and burned up in a large steel tank open at the top. The sawdust from the whole operation was blown to the boiler room, where it was burned in the boiler to furnish steam to run the mill machinery. Some sawmills cut the waste edges into short pieces and sold them for stove or fireplace wood. The sawdust was used in many ways.

When the sawyer had taken enough boards off the log to start squaring it up, he operated a large steam powered mechanical kicker, called

THE LUMBER MILL AND THE MILLPOND
Ford Brothers operated the sawmill for the Rich Lumber Company. Otto Hamele, the author's uncle, was the chief millwright.
(*Courtesy Mr. and Mrs. Robert S. Lansing*)

a nigger, which turned the log over for sawing on the other side. The process was repeated until the log was entirely sawed into the dimensions desired. After the boards were trimmed to standard widths, they continued on to the outside of the mill, where they were piled in the lumberyard. Strips of wood called stickers were placed between layers so that air could circulate and dry out the moisture. When the lumber was properly dried, it was piled on railroad cars and shipped to all parts of the world. At Wanakena a single flat car has been loaded with 43,000 board feet of lumber.

It might be interesting to see how the logs got to the logging railroad which hauled them to the mill. A jobber contracted with the lumber company, for a certain price per thousand board feet, to cut and deliver logs from his assigned area to a designated place along the company railroad or to a rollway along the banks of a stream (in some cases, on the ice of a river). It was stipulated in the contract that the logs had to be at the place designated before the spring thaw, for their value would be very small if they had to remain in the woods until the following year. The jobber went through the tract of woods assigned to him before he made his bid. He knew where he had to build roads, skidways, camps, barns, blacksmith shops, and any other structures for the operation, and of course this information determined the price of his bid. At that time it was no problem to secure workers, and strikes were unheard of. Three types of roads had to be built: the main haul, the tote, and the go-back roads.

First of all, the jobber had to pick a site for the main camp and then start erecting living quarters. As soon as he could, he had a tote road built and maintained on which to haul his tools, food, and supplies into the camp. Large barns were built to house the numerous horses that would be needed, and a well-equipped blacksmith shop was essential. The jobber probably started all this late in April or early May. Soon after, he started the actual cutting of trees. He had to be careful not to cut more trees than could be hauled to the railroad before the next spring's breakup. Other men of his crew had been assigned to build the main haul road and the skidways on which the logs were piled in an orderly manner for easy loading onto the railroad cars with a steam log loader. The main haul road had to be laid out so that it was downgrade or level, for a sleigh-load of green logs was very heavy. If it wasn't possible to design the road without some upgrades, skidways had to be built at the top which were much higher than normal, and which were called double-headers or topping-off skidways. Here the light load of logs which could be hauled up the hill was "topped off" so that the sleigh would be fully loaded for the rest of the trip.

When fall arrived, the main haul road would be completed and waiting for the winter snow. A go-back road was usually built alongside the main haul, but sometimes it would make shortcuts, for it was used only for the empty sleighs as they went back for another load. The roadbeds were ready, but during the winter they would require a great deal of work. When it started to snow, the road builders would start their work by shoveling snow into the low spots and making the road even and smooth. When the temperature dropped below freezing, sleighs loaded with tanks of water were drawn along the road to sprinkle the snow. When the road froze, it would be a fine ice road that would support very heavy loads and, of course, have very little friction for the sleigh runners. The bunks on the sleighs were ten feet wide, and logs were piled on them to a height of eight feet. Yet one team of horses could pull this very heavy load.

When the sleighs were standing still as they were loaded, the runners would eat into the ice so that it would be impossible for the horses to start moving. Men with heavy mauls would pound on the runners to aid the team in loosening them so the sleigh could leave the skidway with its load. Whenever the sleighs were driven over a downhill grade, the horses were pleased, but there was a problem of keeping the sleigh from bumping into and running over the team. At the top or middle of such a grade a shanty was built and stocked with a big pile of sand. Inside the shanty a stove was placed to keep the man tending the hills warm and to keep the sand from freezing. When necessary, the man placed in this job spread just enough sand to keep the sleigh in control but not so much as to make the team work hard.

Whenever there was a snowfall, the snowplows and sweepers had to go to work so as to keep the road clean down to the bed of ice. As one can readily see, it was a lot of work to keep the roadbed in good shape and always usable. The jobbers had the usual midwinter thaw to worry about and always hoped it would be for just a day or two. If there was too much melting, time was lost in building another road. In many cases the men had to be paid even if idle, and the horses had to be fed whether working or not. A long thaw could easily spoil a jobber's chance to make any money and was the big gamble they had to take in agreeing to haul the logs as well as to cut them.

After felling, the trees were cut into standard log lengths, such as ten, twelve, fourteen, and sixteen feet. Some of the large white pine logs

13

were cut into special lengths of over sixteen feet. Good lumberjacks knew just how to fell trees so they would not lodge in other trees and would be easy to cut up into logs without binding the crosscut saw. Like the golfer who hollers "Fore!" just before he tries to hit the poor little ball, the lumberjack bellows "Timber!" just before the tree crashes to earth with its never to be forgotten weird whistling sound. Most of the lumberjacks were paid so much per log, their pay depending upon their skill and speed.

Even before the first snow arrived, the logs were skidded along the ground over previously laid out paths called skidding trails, which were cleared by men called swampers. The horses used for this work became very clever, and with an expert teamster it was most interesting to watch them work handling the logs. They could walk across a railroad trestle with the ties as much as twelve inches apart. If they fell down in the deep snow while skidding a log, they would lie perfectly still, as they had been trained to do, until the teamster unhooked the harness, got out of the way, and then gave them the command to get up. The logs had to be skidded through swamps, uphill, downhill, over sharp rocks, and through streams. The life of the skidding horses was no bed of roses. If the horses became sick, many of the teamsters would sleep all night in the barn with them in order to look after them and give any medicine needed. Lumbering horses were usually all decked out with fancy colored rings and tassels, and their harness shone with polish at all times. The working hours on a log hauling job were from as early as three o'clock in the morning until ten at night, or as long as the horses and men could work out of each twenty-four hours. The horses were rewarded in the spring by being turned out to pasture. The men had to keep working through the blackfly season.

Sometimes the logs were skidded out on the ice of rivers, lakes, or ponds. Or they were piled on the banks and then, when the spring thaw came, they were driven downstream by the river log drivers.

I was fortunate in getting a close-up view of the inside of the sawmill while it was running. I can explain that by telling you that my uncle, J. Otto Hamele, was the chief millwright at the mill. His duties were to keep all the machinery in good running order.

The novelty of watching the machinery soon wore off, so I decided, in addition to being a lumberjack, to become a pond man and walk the logs in the millpond. I purchased a pair of calked shoes and soon had my legs badly cut and bleeding from falling off the logs into the pond. The local kids could run all over the logs with calks on their shoes and of course had a good time laughing at my efforts to keep my feet on the bobbing logs.

The fascination of learning about the lumber mill and log pond and the other facets of logging had kept my desire to go trout fishing in the background, but boy-like I soon began to beg my uncle to take me fishing so that I could try my luck at catching a big trout. I kept after him until he said we could go in a day or two and that he would introduce me to a real Adirondack guide who was a very good friend of his.

3. UP THE OSWEGATCHIE WITH WILFRED

Memories of that first trout breakfast at my grandmother's and stories of big catches finally got the best of me. I asked my grandfather for a shovel to dig some worms. I couldn't believe him when I heard him say, "You have to go to Benson Mines for worms and liquor." Seeing I was confused, he explained that Wanakena was too dry for either item.[3] The village was dry by law and the ground was dry by nature, covered with a layer of duff, made up mostly of conifer droppings, in which fish worms could not thrive.

Carrying my shovel and can, I took the train to Benson Mines and filled a large can with worms while the train was waiting for its mail and passengers. When I returned to Wanakena, I went to the general store and purchased a black and red lumberjack shirt, a reel, plenty of hooks and sinkers, and a pack basket made by real Indians. The basket had leather straps, which were hard to get even in those days.

I was reminded by an old woodsman in the store that I had neglected to buy the three most important items needed for an expedition into the woods. The woodsman was getting a big laugh out of my buying spree, for if the storekeeper had sold me everything I asked for I would have had to have a horse and wagon to tote it. The woodsman told me I needed matches, a compass, and fly dope. I should never forget matches, he said, and I should make it a habit to carry some in a waterproof case. The clerk showed me a nice match case which had a compass on one end and a sunglass on the other and was waterproof. This item, along with the matches and fly dope, was added to my pack of supplies. I left the selection of a fishing rod until the last, for I wanted to ask the guide what rod would be best suited for a beginner. While I was still in the store, my uncle came in with his friend, the renowned Adirondack guide, Wilfred Morrison, and I was introduced to him.

What an impression he made on me at the time! I was sure he must belong to a class of the human race new to me. His eyes were friendly but steel blue, and his grip was so powerful I thought he was going to crush my hand. He stood as straight as a William Tell arrow, was five feet eight inches tall, but to guess his weight would be difficult, for he was as solid and wiry as an otter. His light brown hair was shining under the edge of his old felt hat, his clean-shaven face was smooth and brown like an Indian's, his teeth were slightly stained as a result of the corncob pipe which was his constant companion. His shoulders were so narrow that it seemed there was hardly room for a packsack to ride on them, and his general build was slender. But the natives said he was supple as a string of suckers. He claimed that his birthday fell on Thanksgiving every year, and no one could shake him out of this conviction. The fifty years of his life didn't seem to have taken any toll of his vitality.

I was very excited at meeting such a famous guide, and my admiration grew from that moment on, increasing with each year I knew him. When the introductions were over, Wilfred said, "I'll see you in de morning," and then handed the store clerk a slip of paper and said, "You can put dose ting in my basket and I will get dem tonight. Herbert and I are going in de wood tomorrow."

Five o'clock the next morning found the two of us starting up the Rapids Trail. I guess he noticed I had quite a load, so he made me stop and looked in my pack basket. "My lan," he said, "what you going to do wid so much food? You have enough to last two month." My grandmother knew about my appetite and like all good grandmothers had filled my basket with bread, cookies, cake, and doughnuts, to say nothing of jars of jam and jelly. This weight, added to my already well-stocked supply of canned goods, would have completely exhausted me in a short while if Wilfred hadn't transferred a lot of the food to his basket.

We were still in sight of the railroad bridge, just downstream, when we came to a fish hole called the Wash Hole. The place got its name from the fact that the Italian lumberjacks who camped nearby used it to wash their clothes. They washed clothes by tying them together on the

16

end of a rope and then dropping them into the river, where the churning action caused by the peculiar formation of rocks and water pressure whirled them around and around with an alternating motion just like a modern washing machine. Wilfred said, "Dat is where de Syracuse washer got de idea for dair machine."

We continued to walk up the river on the Rapids Trail, soon coming to a long narrow island. Near the upstream end of the island are located some large boulders, and among them is a place where trout live, called the Brown Trout Hole. Leaving the Brown Trout Hole, the trail went up a slight grade. When we saw the river again, we were some seventy feet above the water looking down at a fish hole known as the Ledges. We found a little fireplace built of stones. From the number of fish heads and bones lying around, it appeared that many tasty meals had been cooked here. The trail now ran downgrade until we were at river level again and saw some large stones in the center of the river supporting a crude log bridge. This was used to walk the skidding horses across when they needed to cross to skid logs out. A good fishing hole called the Bridges is located around these rocks.

The trail again went upgrade and shortly came to a pile of driftwood logs extending out from the shore and held there by rocks in the riverbed. Many large trout have been taken from around these rocks and logs, and of course this is called the Log Pile Fishing Hole. The next place of interest was Little Falls, located just one mile from our starting point at Wanakena. Here there is a drop in the river of some twenty feet, made in two steps. The rocks and the fast water form a very beautiful spot in the river. It is said that more trout have been taken from this place than any other in the Rapids.

At the top of the falls is a stretch of still water approximately a quarter mile long. It ends at another smaller set of rapids or falls. Still water again reaches for another quarter mile to some more short rapids. At the head of these we came to the end of our walking. "Dis is de carry," said Wilfred.

I noticed a smile appear on his face, and when I looked in the direction he was looking, I saw a beautiful Peterborough canoe resting upside down on spruce poles nailed across some trees. He told me to wait and then disappeared in the woods for a few minutes. He soon returned with two handmade hard maple paddles. We put the canoe in the water, and Wilfred put the baskets in the proper spot to help balance the canoe. He showed me how to get into a canoe and gave me a paddle but told me not to use it unless he gave me orders to do so.

STERNBERG'S (INLET HOUSE) IN THE 1890'S
This was the original hotel at Inlet, two miles above Wanakena.
(Courtesy George Sternberg, Jr.)

The first quarter mile was navigated with no talking and nearly silently. I marveled at the ease with which he pushed the canoe along. We went under a footbridge, where the river is shallow and about seventy-five feet wide. These shoals are where the Albany Road, from Albany to Russell and Ogdensburg, once crossed the river. This road was also called the Old Military Road because it was authorized by the State Legislature and partially built during the War of 1812. It was never usable by wheeled vehicles at any one time through its whole length. But many years before I came to the North Woods, early settlers in the town of Fine had used this section of the Albany Road to go to the Plains near High Falls to cut wild hay and haul it back for their stock. In 1907, though, the Albany Road was nothing more than a fishing and hunting trail.

The Albany Trail crossing on the river is known as Inlet, referring to the Oswegatchie as the main feeder of Cranberry Lake, although the crossing is over two miles above Inlet Flow. The rapids downstream make Inlet the natural start of canoe trips on the upper Oswegatchie and a natural rendezvous or campsite in the woods. It is said that arrowheads have been found at Inlet. Indians probably used the route of the Albany Trail for hunting and war parties before the white man ever came to this country.[4]

18

On the northwest bank at Inlet, just above the footbridge, stood a small hotel called Sternberg's or the Inlet House. The beauty and complete peace of mind one experienced there are still very vivid in my memory, although the little hotel and its outbuildings are gone now. Late in 1901, when the Rich Lumber Company made its big land purchase in the township of Emilyville, the twenty-eight acres on which Sternberg's stood were excluded from the deed. Other proprietors followed the Sternbergs, father and son, till the 1960s, when the state bought the little inholding and added it to the surrounding forest preserve.

We went around a sharp bend and found the landing, where several canoes were neatly stored on their racks along with paddles of assorted sizes and lengths. These canoes were rented to anyone the proprietor thought was experienced enough to use them. Wilfred said, "Dis is my headquarter and I guide from here most of de time."

We landed, secured the canoe, and walked to the hotel, where I was introduced to the owner, Mr. George Sternberg. The only way to reach this hotel from the outside was either by the route we had taken or by an old wagon road which started at Star Lake and was called the Walker Road. A garden spot had been cleared near the hotel. Fresh vegetables were served in season. Sternberg's was not subject to the dry laws of Wanakena and Rich Lumber Company lands, so a licensed bar was located in part of the hotel. We went into the barroom, and Wilfred

INLET HOUSE ABOUT 1907
This was the building visited by the author and Wilfred Morrison in 1907. The original hotel had burned, and George Sternberg, Jr., had become the proprietor after his father's death.

said, "Give me a quart of de best," and then gave the bartender a dollar and a quarter. As we started to leave, one of the men at the bar hollered, "Have a drink, Wilfred, before you go?" and Wilfred replied, "Don't mind if I do dat." He then introduced me to a guide by the name of Jack Louden. While the men were drinking, Jack told me about his guiding on the river. When he first started guiding, he said, the falls at High Falls were some fifteen feet further downriver and had worn the rock away that much since he had been guiding. I believed him, of course, until Wilfred told me later it wasn't true. Mrs. Sternberg gave us some coffee and doughnuts, and we shoved off on our thirty-mile canoe trip to the headwaters of the Oswegatchie River.

In about a half mile we came to a spring hole called Thompson's. "Spring hole" is the term used to describe a spot where a spring-fed brook comes into the river or where a spring comes up into the riverbed. At the end of another half mile we came to some swift water, and Wilfred said, "Dese are called Bee Bee Rapid." To get through them with the canoe, we had to follow a very definite channel to prevent damage to the bottom of the canoe. Wilfred shoved the canoe up through this swift water by poling. He always carried a light pole about the length of the inside of the canoe. The pole gave him better leverage than a paddle would and saved the paddle from getting "broomed." I began to realize that it was necessary for one to know the river well to travel it successfully by canoe without hitting rocks and tipping over or ripping holes in the hull.

I was absorbed in watching the scenery as we glided along. Then as we rounded a big bend in the river, Wilfred said, "Dis is de largest bend in de river and is called Big Bend." He showed me a spot where the river narrowed and said, "Dat is a good place to pull out de big one." Ahead of us we could see a nice grove of trees on our left. As we approached them, we saw a camp situated in their midst. Wilfred gave me the information I wanted as he said, "Dat is Maple City Camp, and right ahead is de rapid wid de same name." A little farther, on the right, we came to the outlet of Otter Pond, which is a good fishing pond. This outlet junction is called Otter Creek Spring Hole. Today it is choked with alders, and you must know where it is to find it easily.

We rounded several more bends. When we came to a place where a little creek flowed into the river on the left, I was informed that it was called Dorsey Creek Spring Hole. Next we reached Trapping Shanty Rapids, where an old woodsman once had a camp. One day when he arrived at his camp afoot, he saw a large panther by the boat landing

STRAIGHT OF THE WOODS

Although this photo was taken in August at low water, the river is normally wide and shallow at this point, with masses of water lilies and riverbed grasses waving in the current. The air is heavily balsam scented.

(Courtesy Wesley Hammond)

smelling around inside his canoe. This was supposed to have been the last big cat seen on the Oswegatchie.

We paddled a short distance farther and came to a long, wide section of the river. Wilfred explained, "Dis is called de Straight of de Wood." He shoved the canoe along at a rapid pace in this shallow section by placing his pole on the sandy bottom and shoving, as he had pushed us through the rapids. At the end of this straight he showed me a large white pine on the west bank, which all the guides called the four-mile mark. Next, Wilfred pointed out a rather high bank of red sand and clay on the east shore and said, "Dere is de leaning pine." I strained my eyes but could see nothing but an old stump and some charred roots, for the whole thing had long ago toppled into the stream.

Easy bends, slow bends, sharp bends, rapid bends, and just bends everywhere kept running through my mind till Wilfred remarked, "Here is Jacob Cove, and in high water it is possible to paddle trough it directly to Griffin Rapid, which is where you can see de big green timber, but we will have mile of dese bend to paddle yet." The water was quite

21

HIGH ROCK
The top of the rock commands a long view of Oswegatchie lowlands and is a good place for a lunch break.

(Courtesy Stephen S. Slaughter)

high. I was getting impatient for him to tell me I could use my paddle but didn't say anything about it.

Shortly after leaving Jacob's Cove, I got the long-awaited order to take my paddle and work from the right side. In my anxiety, eagerness, and desire to learn quickly I did everything wrong. The canoe began to shake, for my strokes were too deep, my paddle rubbed on the side of the canoe and twisted and turned at the wrong time. Once I nearly tipped the canoe over when my paddle went through the water edgeways. After about a quarter mile of this Wilfred said, "My lan, I'm glad you do not know anyting about paddling, for you won't have to unlearn any bad habit. I won't let you learn anyting but de right way so dat you will be some use and help to me."

We had a high bank on our left and a very large rock was in view ahead of us. "Dis is High Rock and is five mile from Inlet. We will get out here and look de alder bed over from de top of de rock," Wilfred said as we came to this big rock. At a deep hole in a sharp bend he eased the canoe alongside the rock and up a little brook called High Rock Creek. This spot was rightfully called a good fish catching place. From the top of the rock we could look across a few miles or so of alders and see that the river gently flowed a very crooked route for the next several miles. I could see seven large dead pines in a group about a mile upstream from the rock. Later I found they all grew from one mammoth stump. They were called the Seven Sisters Pines (no longer standing today). Just as we were about to climb down from the rock, we heard a loud splash in the spring hole as if someone had thrown a brick in the water. I asked Wilfred if it was a deer crossing the river and he replied, "My lan no, dat was a trout." I started hurriedly to string up my fishing rod, only to be disappointed when Wilfred said, "We will get de big one for supper tonight, for I like dem to be fresh enough to flop around in de pan."

There seemed to be no use arguing, so we got in the canoe and I started paddling as he told me to. I asked if we could wait a few minutes to see if the big one would jump again, but my request fell on deaf ears and I was told we would soon be where we could see them jumping every few minutes. I didn't really believe him but didn't say anything at all.

We began to get close to the Seven Sisters Pines and then the river swung away. We were soon a quarter of a mile away, only to go back toward them again and then turn away again. Wilfred said, "We will pass dem seven time before we really leave dem. Sometime I tink dey are chasing me." After a while they faded out of sight into the background of the trees and alders, and then we found ourselves right under the branches of a huge white pine. Up on the bank, high and dry, was a beautiful campsite.

"Dis is de Battle Ground," Wilfred said in a low voice. He didn't say anything more for a few minutes, and I began to wonder what battle was fought there. After we had gone around a couple more bends, Wilfred volunteered, "Dere was a couple of guides fought over de ownership of a skiff on dat place." The only additional information I received about the fight was that one had a double-bitted ax and the other an old double-barreled shotgun. To me it appeared everything was "double" and that the fellow with the ax would have the best chance if the old shotgun didn't fire. Wilfred didn't look at it this way. "De fellow wid de ax would not dare take a chance on de udder one pulling de trigger." I never did find out who got the skiff.

23

Wilfred now let me paddle on a few of the bends, giving me orders as to when to paddle and on which side of the canoe. I was sure I wasn't much help, for the canoe didn't seem to go any faster than when I wasn't paddling. I thought about this quite a while. I guess Wilfred knew what I was thinking, for he told me that some of the power in his paddling was lost in having to steer the canoe in the turns and there was always quite a bit of current in these turns. My paddling, when it was done right, helped keep the canoe moving straight without loss of momentum from steering. I began to get the idea, but when the bends were close together it was hard for me not to get mixed up and make a nuisance of myself. Pretty soon Wilfred told me to rest a while.

We came to a deep hole in a bend between high banks, and he remarked, "Dis is de Cherry Hole." I expected him to say it was a good fishing hole, but since he didn't say anything more I asked him about it. He said, "One day coming down de river from de camp with one of my New York City client, Doctuh Cherry, de water was high, and while we were coming round dis bend de doctuh drop his fly rod overboard and de case leak. It didn't float. Later, after de river was down, many looked for dis two hundred dolluh pole, but it was never found."

Hair Bottle Cove, Steve Ward Cutacross, and the Pork Barrel Fish Hole were the places of interest we passed next. Wilfred explained, "De cutacross is where someone cut a little channel wide enough to paddle a canoe from one part of de river to anudder to save going so far. Each spring when de river is high, de rushing water would deepen dis channel. Dis cutacross is named after de fellow who started it, Uncle Steve Ward." In some cases, the river changed and followed the cutacross all the time, so that the old main riverbed was dry except during high water.

I was getting very hungry, so when Wilfred said, "In a few minutes we will be at Griffin Rapid and will eat lunch dere," I was very happy. He told me that there was a good fishing hole there. I was soon to have proof of this statement. Several more bends and we saw a straight stretch of water which led to the foot of Griffin Rapids, about eight miles from Inlet. Just ahead of us we saw a man getting out of a skiff and pulling it up on the shore. Wilfred exclaimed, "I tink it is de Panacake King."

The man turned around, saw us, and waited until our canoe came to the landing and we got out. "Herbert, dis is Mr. John McBroom, a good guide," Wilfred said as he introduced me. The old man showed us four trout, each of which would weigh well over two pounds and one at least three pounds. They had been taken from the fish hole Wilfred had pointed out before. "How would you like to help me eat these?" he asked. When I saw a big smile come over Wilfred's face, I was sure we were going to have a fine dinner instead of dry sandwiches.

We walked a quarter of a mile back into the woods from the river to a fine log camp. Here we rested by getting some dry wood and cutting it into short stove lengths while our host prepared dinner. The camp was located under some very large virgin spruce and hemlock timber.[5] The smell of the trout frying with some real home smoked bacon made my appetite soar to a height never before attained. When we were called to dinner, a large pile of pancakes stood in the center of the table. I wondered who else was coming to dinner. But in an hour nothing of the food remained except a few fish bones and there had been no other guests. I must state right here and now that if any of you readers have never tasted a fresh speckled brook trout dinner amidst the virgin timber in the Adirondack Mountains, you have missed one of the greatest pleasures in life.

While the men were having their after-dinner smoke, the old man told us about a trail called the McBroom Trail, which started at this camp and ended seven miles away at another of his camps. It wound its

GRIFFIN RAPIDS

At high water the rocks in the foreground are well covered, and canoeists are hardly aware of passing through rapids at all.

(Courtesy A. T. Shorey)

way over hills and through valleys and across a long hardwood flat, all the while in thickly wooded country, none of which had ever been lumbered. The camp was beneath a little hill called the Hogsback. Just over this knoll was Wolf Pond, in the middle of several thousand acres of beautiful virgin woods. He invited me to go there with him whenever it was possible.

It was well into the afternoon when we left. Where we had beached the canoe, we were halfway up the rapids, so it took skillful handling to get started without getting crosswise of the stream and thus turning bottom up. Wilfred had the canoe in control at all times, and we were soon at the top of the rapids. "De Panacake King! How do you like his panacake?" he snorted. I said I thought they were wonderful and could understand how he got that name. Wilfred explained, "If we had stayed for supper and breakfast de next morning and even for a week, we would have had panacake for every meal." McBroom was proud of his skill in pancake making. A large prepared pancake flour company paid him a nice sum of money for his recipe. I believe the trade name is seen on many store shelves to this day.

We went just a short distance before we came to another set of short rapids called Stony Rapids. On the right up on the bank was a fine campsite. We could see a skiff tied to the alders. Wilfred murmured, "It look like somebody was home." We climbed out of our canoe, went up the bank, and saw a large man sitting in a comfortable looking chair made of dry spruce poles. He smiled such a welcome that I felt I had been his friend for many years. I couldn't help liking him at first sight. After the introductions Wilfred and I were asked to have supper with him before we went on up the river. He apologized that he didn't have his big tent up yet, so only had sleeping quarters for himself alone. This was his first trip up the river this season, and he would bring in his big tent in a few days. Uncle Steve Ward was a real he-man and a guide who operated from this site, which everyone called Camp Uncle Sam. He was a Civil War veteran. We had a cup of coffee with him, then left, after promising we would return when his big tent was up.

Just after shoving off, we paddled around a bend which just recently had been named the Dad Wilson Fish Hole. Mr. Wilson was an official with the lumber company and was one of the best fly fishermen to wet a fly on the Oswegatchie. He had taken many large trout out of this hole on flies. It was not an uncommon sight to see Dad playing two trout at once, for he always used a three-fly leader. I once saw Dad safely land two trout from the upper pool at Little Falls, each one weighing better than two and a half pounds. Both had been hooked about the same time.

A little farther on we passed an opening in the bank to our right which was called Gouverneur Cove, the entrance to a very dismal looking campsite. You could hear the hedgehogs chewing up this camp clear from the river. Wilfred remarked, "Dat place keep dem away from de udder camp." I said, "Wilfred, you seem to be very fond of Uncle Steve Ward." This must have brought back memories to Wilfred, for he said, "When I was a very young boy, I was sent to live wid a rich uncle in a town in de Province of Quebec, Canada, for my parent, who lived in de eastern part of de Adirondack, had both died. My uncle was very religious, and after I got trough de lower school I was sent to study for de priesthood. When my next vacation came, I decided to visit anudder uncle who lived in Benson Mine. My first uncle didn't like de idea, but I went and when I arrived at Benson Mine on de train, I was very tired and hungry. De uncle dat I was to visit had a very large family, so could only welcome me for a short stay. Job in wood and in de iron mine were only kind at dat time, and I was small and young for dis work, but I decide anyting be better dan going back to de school I hate. My first tought was to get de job so I could stay in de mountain. I learned dere were two popular hotel in town named Ellsworth and de Benson Mine, but all told nine boarding house and saloon where liquor was sold. Some fellow tell me dere were job as choreboy open in a few hotel and lumber camp and told me to try dese place. I asked Mr. Sam Spain, de proprietor of de Ellsworth, for job and he told me he not have one but said de Inlet Hotel was looking for a choreboy and dere would be someone out from dere in a few day. I didn't wait long, for de next morning train have Mr. Sternberg on board, and he hire me for choreboy at de Inlet Hotel. After I work dere bout a week, Uncle Steve come along and ask Mr. Sternberg if he could spare me a few day to help him set up camp. Soon I was sit in front of his guideboat on my way up de Oswegatchie for my first trip. From den on I was call Uncle Steve pupil. My ambition was to be good guide and learn to paddle like Uncle Steve, who could make better time paddling on dis river dan anybody. All guide admire him."

We soon came to Chicken Rapids after rounding an easy bend. On our right we could see the roof of a tar paper covered board camp up on a high bank, halfway up the rapids. Wilfred said, "Dis is de Porter Camp, and we will stay here tonight." On the east side of the river the bank was flat, and tag alders extended for several yards into a newly lumbered swamp. About a half mile through the swamp we could see the logging railroad. The camp where we were was often used by Mr. Royal Ford, one of the Ford brothers who operated the sawmill for the Rich Lumber Company. A canoe was hidden on the side of the river in the swamp so people could cross over to the camp. Since no one was at the camp when we arrived, Wilfred told me to bring our baskets and leave the bait and poles, for we would come back and get some trout for supper.

First thing, of course, was to get some dry wood. We laid it in the stove and poured some kerosene over it. We filled the teakettle and put it over one of the holes left when we took a lid off the stove. I started to light the fire so I could use my new match case, but Wilfred told me to wait until we returned with the trout. He just wanted to get things ready at this time so we wouldn't lose any time when we got back tired and hungry.

We rigged up our poles, got in the canoe, and paddled around a few sharp bends to a place where a little brook, which wended its way across an open meadow, came in. Wham! Splash! Kerplunk! The water suddenly was boiling from the large trout playing and leaping. Could this be a dream? Could they be real trout? Would they bite? Many other crazy thoughts rushed through my head as a really large one threw water right into the canoe. My hands were shaking so that I could hardly bait the hook. Wilfred paddled right across the hole and said, "Dis is Cage Lake Spring Hole, and de little brook is de outlet to Cage Lake, Buck Pond, Panther Creek, and several small brook. De water is very cold."

By the time he had finished talking the canoe was scraping in the mud. I was told to get out and fish from shore. "It's too bad dey are jumping—dey don't bite so good den," Wilfred told me. It was not long before my bait was in front of them, and in less than a minute I had hooked a fairly good sized trout. Now I realized it was a wise choice Wilfred had made to have me pick a good strong steel rod. I pulled the trout onto the shore and was lucky I didn't lose him, for I was too excited to play him at all. "He swallow de sinker too," Wilfred said as he loosened the hook with some difficulty. In a few minutes I hooked another and also snagged him out like a log. Wilfred cleaned the first one while I was catching the second. Then he said, "Dat is enough for tonight, and in de morning we will eat bacon and egg."

In less than an hour from the time we had fixed the wood in the stove, we were eating 2½-pound trout with fried potatoes, cake, cookies, jam, and jelly and washing it down with good hot tea. Five minutes after I had wiped the dishes, I was fast asleep. If any wild animals came around during the night, I didn't hear them. An old chattering alarm clock with no paint on the dial woke me, and I smelled the aroma of coffee coming from the kitchen and heard a voice calling me to breakfast. The bacon and eggs tasted very good. As I ate, Wilfred asked me to do the dishes while he cut wood to replace what we had used. This was one phase of woods life Wilfred never forgot. Everyone likes to find a nice box of dry wood when he comes to a camp, and especially if it is raining. Few people ever think to replace what they have enjoyed.

Eight o'clock found us once more paddling through Cage Lake Spring Hole, which is about eleven miles from Sternberg's. This time the trout were very quiet. We navigated a few more bends and found we were looking into a large opening on the right side of the river. "Dis is Rock Cove. In high water we could paddle right over de bank at de end of de cove and save a few bend," Wilfred told me. Before long we came to a bad, knotty log embedded in sand on the river bottom close to the channel. This log was called Sternberg's Snag, for here at one time Mr. Sternberg ripped a long hole in the bottom of a new canoe he had just purchased. Next we came to a large hardwood saw log on the bottom of the stream almost across the channel. There was just room for us to get through. This was called Gates's Log, taking its name from Walter Gates. One day when a few guides were coming up the river for the spring cleaning out of snags and logs, Walter was standing on this log, which was about sixteen inches under water, chopping and floating debris. He slipped and fell into the water up to his neck. The log is still there today. When it is entirely covered, you know that you can make Round Hill Rapids.

A few bends later we saw a large boulder almost in the center of the stream, and Wilfred told me it was called Leo's Rock. It got this name from one of John McBroom's small boys, who was fishing with his father one day but wouldn't sit still in the canoe. His father made him sit on this rock until he finished fishing. After unwrapping a few more bends, we saw another large boulder in the river with a balsam fir growing on its top, so of course it was called Balsam Rock.

We bucked a very strong current for the next half mile till we came to Buck Cove. Over the marsh land on the left we could see the logging railroad. In a little while we came to a spot where a small brook flowed into the river. Here we pulled the canoe up on a sandbar, and Wilfred proudly exclaimed, "Dis is de Wilfred Morrison Spring Hole." As I looked at the entanglement of old sunken logs, I thought it didn't amount to much, for I was sure one couldn't land a big trout safely out of it. We saw some large buck deer tracks on the sandbar, and Wilfred said, "He just left before we came around de bend." I asked him how he knew, and he told me to step on the sand near the buck track and then get back in the canoe. "Now watch how fast de color change," Wilfred said. You could easily see the rapid fading of the moisture as the hot sun dried out the track.

Several more bends and we came to a wooden dam across the river. Here was built what was called the Jack Works. A spur from the railroad came to the river bank. The land on both sides of the river was owned by the Rich Lumber Company. A dam, along with three more built further up river, backed the water up high enough so it was possible to float logs down to this spot clear from High Falls. The end of the dam was left open so the trout could get around. We pulled our canoe through this gate of water and found that the river was now much deeper and had long stretches without bends.

On one large bend a lot of flood wood was boomed so it couldn't get away, and at the side there was a spot cleared out which was called New York Landing. A party from New York City had camped there for so many years that the spot finally took this name. Many large trout were caught under the shade created by the logs held in this pool. We soon entered another fairly long straight section, and Wilfred said, "We will soon be dere." I searched both banks looking for it, for I knew he was proud of his camp and I wanted to recognize it when we got there. As we paddled by, I saw it on the wide part of a large bend up on high ground. We beached the canoe on the landing, and as we walked up to the cabin Wilfred said with a smile, "Herbert, dis is Camp Betsy."

4. CAMP BETSY

The camp was a nice two-story structure with a comfortable looking roofed-over front porch. The view from the porch was up and down long straight parts of the river with beautiful evergreen trees on both banks. There was a long sloping hill which ran up from the rear of the cabin, and a wonderful cold spring was nearby, along with lots of hard birch wood for the stoves. The logging company had given Wilfred sole use of the camp for the many favors he had done for them and also for showing their surveyors around the property that he knew so well.

There was a large iron kettle in the front yard. Wilfred built a smudge fire in it, and it wasn't long before there were very few punkies, black flies, or mosquitoes in the area. We went to the spring for water and soon had dinner ready. After the meal and after the dishes had been washed, wiped, and put away, I looked around and found many cans of food in the pantry. I asked Wilfred if he ever had any of his things stolen, for I had noticed there was no lock on the cabin. "If dey ever take any ting, dere will be a note say dey will be replace or de money for more left someplace in town." He went on to tell me that very few people came in the woods or up the river without a guide anyway.

We went out on the porch and sat in some comfortable chairs while we talked. Once in a while we could see trout jumping in the river. Finally Wilfred suggested that we cut some wood, as it looked as if it might rain before morning.

I asked Wilfred how Camp Betsy got its name. He was not married then or later, and I knew of no woman in his life. He told me that he had named the camp in honor of the wife of one of his clients.

Wilfred taught me many things. He told and showed me the things one needed to know to be a good guide. He taught me how to grind and sharpen a double-bitted ax, how to chop and saw wood, how to file and fit a crosscut saw, how to paddle a canoe and handle other kinds of boats, and how to administer first aid. The most important thing he taught me was that, to be a good guide, you must always be courteous and gentlemanly, for your conduct may determine whether a customer ever returns or recommends you to his friends. I had secretly determined that I wanted someday to become a guide.

We cut the necessary amount of wood that afternoon, and while Wilfred got the supper I was given the job of carrying the wood into the shed attached to the back of the cabin. When supper was over and the dishes washed, I began to realize that there was lots of hard work attached to this camping business. We spent the remainder of the evening repacking our pack baskets, for Wilfred had said we would go on up the river in the morning.

The night seemed only a few minutes long when I heard Wilfred with his "Breakfast is ready" call. We were part way down the path to the canoe when he sent me back after the canoe paddles. He explained that they were specially made by hand and he seldom left them outside, as he had when we first got the canoe. He also explained that porcupines chew on anything which has a salty taste and of course would ruin the sweat-impregnated handle of a paddle. His paddles were called Chase paddles after the man in Fine, New York, who made them by hand. This man had won first prize with his paddles at one of the world fairs. Since he was getting to be an old man, his paddles were more prized than ever by their owners. My uncle, Mr. Hamele, had two of them, with one made of bird's-eye maple and the other of black cherry wood. My uncle thought so much of these paddles that he never would use them and kept them hung on the wall of his home as one would a famous painting. Many other Adirondack paddle makers tried to imitate them but could never quite get the grip to feel right.

We stopped at the camp spring, which was near the landing, pulled some tufted moss which grew around it, and repacked our bait cans so the worms would keep well. As we started upstream and rounded a bend, Wilfred said, "We are now coming into de aristocrat section of de big speckled trout world. De next seven mile have never been equaled anywhere in America for having so many large speckled trout." Nowhere else has any stream or any portion of it, so it is said, been able to produce such a feeling of longing to return year after year once one has been over its course. Its magic spell makes one forget his troubles, business, and ills and completely relax. Relaxation and refreshing sleep enable one to arise feeling glad to be alive and better prepared for life. Rich man, poor man, young and old, famous and unknown all meet on equal terms in this paradise from Camp Betsy to High Falls. No one talks business, and position in life is unimportant when one contemplates nature's handiwork just as God planned it should be.

As we approached the foot of Ross Rapids, we heard the screeching of the railroad car wheels on the logging train. The railroad tracks were laid close to the north bank of the rapids at this point. "Dat noise is de death knoll for all dat I just tol you about dis section" was Wilfred's sad remark. We beached the canoe, got out, and walked up a narrow path leading to the grade. Climbing up, we could see a box fastened on a big tree with the words "Camp Betsy" written on it. "Dis is de mailbox. De engineer bring our mail up every morning, so we will wait and see if dere is any today," Wilfred explained.

The old Shay geared locomotive came to a grinding, screeching stop with its string of empty log cars behind, and the engineer gave Wilfred some papers and a note which said he should go to Wanakena and call the New York telephone operator at once. The engineer said the train would be going down about two o'clock and Wilfred could ride with

SITE OF CAMP BETSY TODAY
The camp, which was destroyed when the state acquired the land, commanded a view up and down river from its location at the outer side of a bend.

(*Courtesy Wesley Hammond*)

them and return early in the morning. My friend thanked the engineer, and we started back down the path to the canoe.

Just as we swung out into the center of the stream, a large trout jumped at the head of the rapids. "Dere is our dinner. We will go get him," Wilfred exclaimed with real eagerness in his voice. He paddled up through the rapids and partly around the big bend. There we stopped to see if the big trout would jump again. When a reasonable length of time had passed with no sign of the trout, Wilfred commented, "Dat is fine, he is waiting for his breakfast," and then he moved the canoe very slowly to within casting distance of the top of the rapids. I was told to cast the bait as far as possible straight ahead. My line was dry, which helped me in my inexperience to get some distance in my cast. But the cast fell short by a few yards. I heard a sigh from the stern of the canoe. I felt bad till all of a sudden the line shot off the reel at a terrific speed. My hands felt paralyzed. My line snapped where the end was tied to the reel, and a streak in the still water was all I could see of the fish.

I heard my friend say, "Ha, ha, ha, dat was more fun dan if you save

33

him." I was relieved that Wilfred could laugh and save me from such an embarrassing moment. He shoved the canoe to shore and pawed through his pack basket until he located a brand new fish line, which he handed to me with the words, "Don't let dat happen again." It was with shaking hands that I wound the new line on my reel and, while doing so, made up my mind I would always have control of my line after losing such a man-sized trout as this one. It had given me a lesson.

I put on a new hook, a sinker, and a large night crawler and was all set for the second act. I threw in the bait, and as it began to sink a swell appeared with lightning speed. In an instant my rod was bowed clear down to the water. I forgot I was in a canoe and stood up to better fight this prize. Then I heard, "By de Jeez," just before my head entered the water and my feet pointed at the sky. I swam the few feet to shore, stood up, shook the water out of my eyes, and discovered Wilfred holding my pole and calmly playing a large trout. I had thrown the pole right into his hands as I waved my arms trying to keep my balance. The trout had swallowed the hook and was soon safely landed.

All Wilfred had to say about my foolishness was, "My lan, what a performance for just a two-pound trout." I guess he thought my schooling was over for the day, for he picked me up and paddled us with all the skill, grace, and ease of an Indian guide down through the rapids and on to camp.

The two-pound trout, as Wilfred called it, was more than enough for our dinner. I was sure that if it could have been weighed, it would have been closer to three pounds. Wilfred told me I could go to Wanakena with him if I was afraid to stay alone in the woods, but I decided to stay and practice canoe paddling while I was waiting to continue our trip up the river. Wilfred advised me not to take the canoe around bends in the river where the water was deep and fast. He gave me a burlap bag and told me to put enough sand in it to balance the canoe as if another person were in the boat with me. We paddled up to the foot of Ross Rapids, where Wilfred left me to catch the log train, which I could hear chugging along with its cars of logs.

I was very anxious to try paddling alone, so I hurriedly filled the bag with sand and put it in the front of the canoe. I found that the canoe balanced very nicely. Then I remembered another thing Wilfred had said, "Don't rub de side with de paddle! Don't rub de side with de paddle!" This warning kept ringing through my ears. Rubbing the paddle was one evil that Wilfred just wouldn't tolerate. He always said he could tell when some "hop-sooner" used his canoe.

34

I paddled several hours. Finally my appetite overcame my enthusiasm for canoeing. I soon had supper cooking on the stove. When eight o'clock arrived, I could hardly keep my eyes open and soon was fast asleep. Wilfred, who was a great collector of alarm clocks, had evidently wound and set them before he left, for just about daybreak they all went on a rampage. I made a few extra cups of coffee, for Wilfred had told me he expected to eat breakfast with me when he returned. I met the logging train, and my friend and I paddled back to camp in double time. He told me that his telephone call was to let him know a party would arrive the first of July. He was to guide them from this camp.

5. HIGH FALLS AND BEYOND

I was glad to hear our excursion up the river was to continue. We got started right away. When Wilfred shoved the canoe through Ross Rapids, several lumberjacks were watching from the bank. He didn't let it slip back even one inch, and I noticed the smile of approval on their faces. Several rocks in these rapids are right in the only spot you can use. Today they are well aluminized from keels and outboard propellers hitting them.

Just across the railroad grade there was a large boulder which must have weighed over twenty tons and looked as though it might roll onto the track at any moment. When the people who used the railroad track went by it, they used to say, "Well, the next time we go by here the road will be blocked." On the south bank of the river at the first bend above the rapids stood a tar paper camp used by a Mr. Livingston, from New York City, who also had a similar camp a mile and a half down the river from Wanakena. The latter was located at the mouth of a little stream called the Livingston Spring Hole.

After making the bend, we came onto a straight. At the upper end we could see a large rock near the center of the river which was usually just a few inches below the surface. This was called Mrs. Brown's Rock because she drove her canoe up on it and was grounded there until her husband, a doctor, came along and helped her get free. All through this

35

GUIDE AND PARTY ON THE OSWEGATCHIE
Mrs. Doc Brown, for whom Mrs. Brown's Rock was named, holds a good catch as Wilfred Morrison stands in the stern of his Peterborough canoe.

long second bend large boulders just under the surface made it a good trout hole. As we continued around the U-shaped bend, we passed a wonderful campsite on the north shore beside a spring brook. This place was called Camp Ideal and Camp Ideal Spring Hole. A famous guide from Star Lake by the name of Ed Young camped here with his parties for many years. Here large trout were jumping, and Wilfred said, "It will be like dis for de rest of de summer."

Ahead of us, after completing the bend, was a long set of rapids called Straight Rapids. At their foot is located the deepest spot in the river. The next bend is called Rocky Bend, well named for its many hidden rocks. Proceeding on for a short distance, we came to the bank on our right where a little dry canal cuts across to the river on the other side and is about three boat-lengths long. We went on to a sharp bend in thick timber where is located a famous fishing hole called the Old Glory Hole. For many years many large trout were caught here. Bearing around sharp left, we came to the opposite end of the little dry canal, which is used in high water for a short cut. The tannin-stained water is beautifully smooth here. Another bend brings us to Gates's Fish Hole. Swinging through an S-bend, we arrived at a deep spot called the Root Hole, where an enormous pine root was embedded in sand. About 1911

36

this big stump with its octopus roots washed out of the bank in high water and trundled away. After hanging up on some alders and staying in place for about fifteen years, it resumed its slow journey downstream with each year's spring runoff. Finally, it reached the Inlet landing in the spring of 1967. At this writing it is still there, its roots providing many-leveled seats for picnickers about to launch their boats. Parts of it have been cut off for firewood. Someday it may float down through the Rapids and reach Cranberry Lake.

A few hundred yards above the Root Hole we came to a large bend into which a clear stream with a white sandy bottom riffled. "Dis is Wolf Creek Spring Hole. I tink it is one of de most beautiful spot on de river," said Wilfred. To me it looked like the best place to fish, and had I been a trout I would have picked this spot for my summer home. Wilfred said that a good catch of trout was assured here almost any time you cared to fish for them. Diagonally across the bend from the mouth of the creek, on the same side, was a landing used by people going to Five Ponds, which are about three miles south of the river. In later years I never passed this place without dreaming of the headwaters of Wolf Creek, all in virgin forest in northeast Herkimer County.[6] One of the highest sources is beautiful Streeter Fishpond, whose water is so clear you can see the bottom at a depth of forty feet. The outlet of Streeter feeds Wolf Pond, the largest body of water on the Wolf Creek chain. After flowing through Big Five and Little Five, the creek is joined, at the north end of a hogback ridge or esker of huge white pines, by the outlet of Little Shallow and Big Shallow of the Five Ponds group.

Left, right, left, right came the bends all during the next mile. Then we arrived at the most beautiful set of rapids on the river. They are called Round Hill Rapids and are the most difficult to paddle through either up or down stream. Only a few of the guides attempted to push a canoe up through these rapids. When Wilfred gave the canoe a final shove at the top of the rapids, my heart started to beat normally again. I began to wonder if there was anything he could not do with a paddle, a pole, and a canoe. At this point was a pretty little footbridge spanning the stream. On the south side on a high flat spot was a large lumber camp called Walter Moore's Camp. A little round hill rising up from the rear of the buildings gave the rapids their name.

With a chuckle Wilfred said, "Walter drink quite a lot when he is out of de wood. One day when he was in Tupper Lake he went to see a doctuh. Walter said wid his mouth open, 'Doc, look down my troat.' After taking a good look, de old sawbone said, 'Dar is nutting wrong

LINING A CANOE THROUGH ROUND HILL RAPIDS
These are the most difficult rapids above Inlet to paddle through. They are shown here at low water.

(Courtesy A. T. Shorey)

wid your troat.' Walter grunt and say, 'Dere ought to be, dere is two farms and tree big lumber job down dere.' "

We made a left bend beyond the bridge into a straight of about one hundred yards. Another bend brought a longer straight into view, and near the end of it we came to a pretty spot known as Crooked Rapids. Lots of big tamarack trees grew on both banks of the river. Very soon we came to another set of rapids called Sugar Rapids. They got their name from the fact that a guide, George Preston, tipped over his canoe loaded with a barrel of sugar. He had paddled all the way up from Inlet, some eighteen miles, and was only a few hundred feet from the end of the trip.

In a few minutes Wilfred exclaimed, "Here is de champion of dem all. Carter Spring Hole." At the point of an L-shaped bend was a landing spot called Carter's Landing. A tiny creek, the outlet of Moses' Rock Spring, flowed into the river nearby. Just above this point and on the same side a cold brook also flowed into the river. It is called Glasby Brook and is the outlet of Glasby Pond, which is several miles to the northeast. These two inlets bound the main part of the Oswegatchie known as Carter's Spring Hole. Hundreds of large trout have been caught in the portion of the river about two hundred yards above and below this spring hole. The log railroad ran along part of this L-shaped bend. Thick heavy alders grew out of the water's edge and along both banks. To land a big trout safely without getting snagged was a feat not easily accomplished. On the north shore a little way up the side of a hill was a grand campsite. Looking up the winding river from this point, Carter's Plain, now called simply the Plains, stretched out to the east with its hundreds of beautiful tamaracks, over the top of which one could see Three Mile Mountain.[7] The south side of the river had a beautiful background of thick dark timber rising gently in its climb to the sky. Looking east from the landing on the railroad, one could see Cat Mountain, several miles away, with its high old wooden fire observation tower.

Cornelius Carter [8] was a well-known guide in this section before 1900, and the plains and spring hole derived their names from him. He patrolled this property before the Rich Lumber Company purchased it. There is a deep hole beside a large rock at the top of Ross Rapids which is called Carter's Magic Fish Box, for Carter appeared to be the only person who could catch big trout out of this hole whenever he wanted to fish there. Several of the guides used to tell of seeing him go to this spring hole with a long stick and whip the alders for several minutes, bait up, and then with a stiff tamarack pole jerk trout as soon as they were hooked.

CARTER'S CAMP ON THE PLAINS ABOUT 1890
Cornelius Carter stands in front of his log cabin on the Plains. The larger building is his guest house.

(Courtesy George McAlister)

After leaving Carter's Landing, we had one bend after another for the next mile. A high smooth-faced rock on the south shore called Moss Rock is a landmark in this section. Its straight side rises above the river like a wall to a height of fourteen feet. The different high water marks formed each year are plainly visible on it. From the top, one has an overlook of the whole area.

After several more bends and straights had been rounded, we arrived at High Falls. Wilfred said, "De big trout are so anxious to get to High Fall dey don't stop along de way, so only small one are caught up to High Fall."

Some visitors have said that whoever named High Falls must have known only the upper Oswegatchie. The waterfall is only about twenty feet high. But if the name is slightly misleading, any disappointment experienced by a person seeing the falls for the first time is quickly overcome by the beauty of the setting. That is the way it was with me on this first visit to High Falls with Wilfred.

A glistening sheet of water foamed and sprayed down into a cool deep pool which extended back under the rock formation farther than a long pole would reach—a big trout Garden of Eden. The water took on

HIGH FALLS
The big trout that used to try to jump the falls are gone, but small ones are still caught here.

(*Courtesy Dwight Church*)

new life as it eased over the edge of a five foot shelf into another lovely pool and finally leveled off into a white dotted surface. Mammoth virgin white pine towered as sentinels on each side of the river, backed by dark green walls of spruce, balsam, and hemlock.

I had almost forgotten to breathe while taking all this in, and now I inhaled lungs full of a kind of air I had never breathed before—air coursing down the river on a south breeze, cooled by the cold water, bearing the spicy odors of a great conifer forest.

"I am very glad," said Wilfred, "dat de company decide not to cut dese big pine around dis place." At the beginning of the smooth water below the falls a little log camp stood among the pines. There was a large camp at the top of the falls which was used by the boss jobbers. Large trout were continually trying to jump the falls. Their leaps sometimes attained a height of six to eight feet, but none was ever able to make it.[9] Above the falls a wooden bridge had been constructed across the river and a log road built one mile to the Herkimer County line and the virgin timber of the forest preserve.

We carried our canoe and camping equipment around the falls to a little bay extending back from the river at a safe distance from the brink. We launched the canoe there and paddled out into the main stream. Wilfred said, "From here de river gradually get smaller, and in nine or ten mile it will be just a few small spring brook." No trout longer than twelve inches were caught above the falls, he told me. The average length ran about nine inches. But these small trout could be caught almost anywhere.

Red Horn Creek was the first landmark we came to, just north of the St. Lawrence County line. It came in on the left. So too did Nicks Pond Outlet, about a mile south of the line in Herkimer County. Near here, at a bend in the river, was a narrow little knoll called Camp Johnny. Behind it, a few hundred feet across a swale and beneath a ridge, was a spring with water so cold it would make your teeth chatter if you drank too much at a time. If you had wanted to design a pleasant camping place in the virgin forest with all you could think of to make it perfect, you could have done no better.

Almost everyone who camps at Camp Johnny has some story to tell about it. A few years ago my friend Wes and his wife, whom I became acquainted with by shortwave radio and lured to the Oswegatchie for several vacations, made a trip to Camp Johnny. During the night raccoons kept them awake. About daylight Wes got up, built a fire, and started breakfast. While engaged in this, he felt something brush against his legs. Turning, he saw a bear cub scamper to the base of a tall white pine and climb thirty feet, where it came to rest on a dead limb. Suddenly the limb broke. The young cub tumbled through the air but managed to grab the tree trunk before hitting the ground. It made quite a noise. Wes expected the mother bear to come to the rescue, but she stayed back in the swale and called her cub, which eased onto the ground and ran to its mother. Wes only had time to get a color photo of the cub.

Wilfred shoved the canoe over to the landing and we got out. We went up the little trail to the camp and sat for a while gazing around at the beautiful surroundings. "We will go over to Pine Ridge," Wilfred said; "I want to see de big pine." Heading east from Camp Johnny, we crossed a grassy swamp past the spring and climbed the side of a small steep hill. Here were hundreds of virgin white pine towering into the sky. Wilfred explained that they extended along the ridge as far as the Little Plain and were known as the largest stand of virgin white pine in the United States. In the early 1920s, the day of silent movies, a film company chose this location for a setting in primeval forest which they needed. They spent a month or two on Pine Ridge making a film which old residents in Wanakena remember as "the Daniel Boone picture." [10]

Standing among the big pines and hemlocks, I understood where some of that invigorating odor given off by the spray at High Falls came from, for nothing could traverse this country without gathering something to smell from those magnificent trees. Wilfred remarked on the way back to the canoe, "De smell of dis country make me feel so I can shove de canoe a rod wid every stroke."

Paddling on for nearly a mile, we came to the Robinson River, entering on the right, which looked almost as large as the Oswegatchie itself at this point. A short way up the main stream from the mouth of the feeder was a pretty stretch of rough water called the Robinson River Rapids. Near these rapids, on a rise of ground, stood a snug little log camp complete with dishes, stove, and cooking utensils. Wilfred told me that several different guides claimed to have built it, but since no one was there, he said, "We will stay here tonight." Two guides named Greenfield and Schuyler operated from this section before 1902 and had log camps near the rapids. A mountain near here, between the Robinson River and Gal Pond, was named after Greenfield.

We cut some wood and put it in the stove in preparation for supper, as we had done at Chicken Rapids. "We will go and get some nice little trout for supper," remarked Wilfred, as he filled the old copper tea kettle. "De trout will be small and you do not have to worry about losing de line." At the foot of the rapids we soon caught enough for supper. I suggested we catch some for breakfast, but Wilfred said, "No, I like dem to flop in de pan." The smallest of the trout were fried very crisp, and my friend ate them head, tail, and all.

Once during the night a hedgehog started gnawing on the camp door. Wilfred got up and hit him with a club, and then everything was peaceful for the rest of the night. When I awakened early in the morning, I smelled the coffee boiling and saw Wilfred put some flopping trout into the frying pan. He had been out early and caught enough for breakfast. I felt like a new person after the wonderful night of sleep, the delicious meal, and all. I decided right then and there I was going to spend as much of my life as possible in these great woods.

After we had cleaned up the dishes, Wilfred said, "Today we will go to de headwater and come back here again tonight." As we paddled up the river, we saw several very desirable campsites. About noon the river got so small and narrow we could no longer paddle the canoe. Here it fanned out into little spring brooks. We had arrived at the end of our thirty-mile trip. While eating lunch, my friend remarked, "Dis will be a good place for de beaver to build a dam when dey get back in dis part of de wood." [11] As we were about to start back, a train whistle could be faintly heard several miles away to the east. It was from the old Mohawk and Malone Railroad, or Adirondack Division of the New York Central. Wilfred said, "I hope dat is de nearest any mechanical driven contraption ever get to dis place."

When we started downstream, Wilfred placed the baskets and luggage in the canoe so as to sink the front end slightly more than when we had gone upstream. This enabled him to swing the stem around more easily with the current on some of the fast bends. Little effort was required to keep the canoe moving, but plenty was used in making the fast water bends. I received more instructions on assisting around these bends. Wilfred said, "On de average it take about twice as long to paddle up de stream on dis river as it do going down." We stopped at the foot of Robinson River Rapids and caught enough trout for our supper. "What is next?" asked Wilfred, and I replied, "Cut wood." "Dat is right," he said, "for no matter how many year of your life is spent in de wood, big part of de time is spent in cutting de wood to cook and for keeping warm in de cold weather."

After another night of restful sleep in the deep woods we headed downstream again. About a mile above High Falls on the north side of the river we came to a high bank where many logs were piled. "Dis is de banking ground," Wilfred said, "and someday dey will have de river full from here to de Jack Work." The large trout were jumping and playing at High Falls as we carried our canoe around them.

We made very good time in getting back to Camp Betsy. Wilfred was pleased with my offer to help him cut enough wood to last while his party was at camp. Starting from the rear of Camp Betsy, there was a trail which led up over the hill and joined the main trail from Round Hill Rapids to Big Shallow Pond. We spent one day cutting the grass and brush on it and clearing out fallen trees.

After a few days we started downstream for Inlet and Wanakena. I wanted very much to take back a mess of large trout to show my uncle. Wilfred said, "We will get a few out of de best place as we go along." Cage Lake Spring Hole was as calm as a sheet of glass at this early hour. Wilfred stopped the canoe several yards before reaching the edge of the pool. "I will tell you when to trow in de bait," he said, as he fixed a branch of alder to sit on and thus hold the canoe. "Let de bait float carefully down from in front of de boat and den be ready to snub a big un," Wilfred whispered. Hardly had he finished the sentence when my line tightened. Readers who have had such an experience with a large trout know the thrill which goes through one and leaves exciting memories that are never forgotten. Wilfred quickly shoved the canoe across the hole onto the flat shore, where I was able to land safely my 2¾-pound speckled beauty. When I held him up with the cool spring water dripping from his sides, the morning sun brought forth the rapidly changing glorious colors that nature had so artistically placed there, and I was sure no artist would ever dare to try and imitate this beauty. "Dat is enough for here. We will get some more at anudder place," Wilfred said.

Our next try was at the Dad Wilson Fish Hole, where a similar performance was enacted. This time I had a two-pounder. "We will get one at High Rock and anudder at de Otter Creek Spring Hole, and den you will have enough to satisfy your uncle dat you can catch de big one," remarked Wilfred, as we left and swung around into Stony Rapids. The next hour found us at High Rock Spring Hole, and here I missed a trout which would have weighed over four pounds. This trout must have put a jinx on me, for in over forty years of fishing the Oswegatchie I never saved a trout weighing more than three and a half pounds.

Even Wilfred got excited when I hooked this one, and he kept begging me to keep the slack out of the line. He picked up the old landing net from the bottom of the canoe and found it was rotten and full of holes. "By de Jeez! I either leave de landing net at camp or just have a barrel hoop in de boat," he exclaimed as he saw the net was useless. He backed the boat onto a sandbar and got out, saying, "Bring him over to me very careful, and when I take de line let go de slack." Being excited and anxious, I pulled too hard and all was over in a flash. A little piece of skin on the hook told the sad story. "Dat will learn you a lesson," Wilfred said. "Never forget. It don't pay to hurry dem," as he shoved the canoe, in a burst of angry speed, into the stream and on down the river.

When we came to Otter Creek Spring Hole, Wilfred said, "I will give you one more chance and dat is all." When he had the canoe in the right place, the word to throw in was given. The sun was pretty high and it did not look as though we would get another strike before evening. But after about thirty minutes a two pounder grabbed the bait and soon was safely in the boat.

Another hour of paddling brought us to the carry. It seemed good to hit the trail for a change and thus stretch our legs. We didn't leave the paddles in the woods this time but carried them with us to town. My three large trout were admired by my uncle, and he was well pleased with my account of the trip.

The summer soon slipped away as summers have a habit of doing. Another trip into the woods with my friend would have to wait until next year. My last day before leaving for home and school was happily spent in fishing at Livingston Spring Hole on the Flow. I caught several large trout, and my grandmother fried them for me to pack with my lunch. When I boarded the train early the next morning, I felt like a real guide with my pack basket, lumberjack shirt, pair of real calked lumberjack shoes, and bear paw snowshoes. For once I didn't eat everything but kept the fried trout to show the boys at home. At first, none of the boys believed I had caught the trout. I gave samples to so many people that they didn't last long.

I was anxious to try out the new snowshoes. On the first day we had two inches of snow I walked to school with them on.

6. FOREST FIRES

It was June again, and I left for the Adirondacks. When I arrived at Benson Mines, the train was about an hour late and it was dark, but there was a large crowd of excited people at the station. A tremendous forest fire was raging in the woods for several miles around. Every able-bodied man was doing what he could to battle the flames, which were at that time some distance from Wanakena. In a few days the major fires were under control, but all that summer of 1908 the weatherman poured on the heat. Rainfall was below normal, and the slashing from previous lumbering got dry enough to burn fiercely.

The Rich Lumber Company hired many extra men to patrol the woods and encouraged workers to be extra careful with matches and fires of any kind. Some of the men who loved this section of the country and wanted it kept in its native state were angry that it was being lumbered off. They had remarked that when the tops got dry enough there would be a hot time in the forest. Those remarks got back to company officials, who hired some of the angry men, at a good salary, to help prevent fires and to lessen complaints.

The log trains were run only at night, when the dew was on, to prevent sparks from the coal burning locomotives from setting more fires. At every wooden trestle barrels of water were placed to be handy in case of need. A large flatcar was equipped with a water pump operated by steam from the locomotive, and water tank cars were constructed. Many hundreds of feet of fire hose were placed on these cars, and a long siphon hose to get water from streams near the railroad was also carried.

All the mill and woods workers were alerted. The atmosphere around town was like waiting for a long fuse to burn into a keg of powder. Some of the townspeople dug deep holes to bury their valuables in if necessary, and many other means of protection were figured out. Careful watch was kept to prevent anyone from going into the woods without permission. Every few days a small fire would start but was quickly put out. On some days smoke from large fires in the Canadian woods drifted down into this area and gave the town a ghostly appearance.

46

A REST STOP

Resting at the Porter Camp at Chicken Rapids on a hike to Sand Lake in 1908 are (from left) J. Otto Hamele, Willie Stewart, and the author. Another hiker, Henry Wells, took the picture. *(Courtesy Henry Wells)*

My friend Wilfred was very busy guiding. He had been engaged for the entire summer season by some wealthy people from Buffalo and New York City. During the previous winter he had accepted an invitation to spend considerable time at a client's Florida home. Now he had a lot to tell about his experience in high society. His camp was full of guests. He, another guide, and a cook the party had brought with them stayed in a tent near the landing. I was very happy when Wilfred asked me to help him paddle a load of provisions and baggage up to his camp and then learned there was room for me to sleep in the tent with the guides.

This summer, without a doubt, turned out to be the best season for real trout fly fishermen that the river had ever seen. Several guides were operating camps above High Falls, a large camp was doing business at High Falls, others at Carter's old campsite and at Boiling Spring on the Plains were prospering, and several more scattered along the river below the Jack Works were in business. When the guides began to come upriver after the peak of the Rapids fishing at Wanakena was over, they

47

found the river above the Jack Works full of logs from shore to shore and as far as Moss Rock, a distance of nearly four miles. Thousands of logs had been dumped into the river to be floated down to the Jack Works, where they would be taken out and loaded on the railroad cars. A great fight began between the guides and the Rich Lumber Company and their jobbers. The guides won out and the river was boomed with logs to leave a passageway for canoes and boats. Most of the guides and other sportsmen predicted that this section of the river would not be any good for fishing, so the situation looked rather gloomy for Wilfred and his parties.

During my first trip up the river that summer, Wilfred told me how disappointed he was with his trip to Florida. "My lan, I tought I was going to eat wid de help," he told me as we left the landing at Inlet. "Dey told me, 'You are our guest, Wilfred, and are not here to work or eat wid de help.' When I got to de table, dere was so many tool I didn't know which one to use. I watched dem very careful and I was alway just a little behind dem, but could soon handle de tool like an old society buck. One day de Miss said, 'Wilfred, where did you learn to have such good manner? Why, your table manner are better dan most of my guest.'" I doubted that Wilfred had learned all his manners on his Southern trip, for he had always had a reputation of being one of the most polite and gentlemanly guides on the river.

One notable act of Wilfred's was to peel a soft-boiled egg with a knife at the breakfast table. Many times he was served a soft-boiled egg for breakfast just so his artistic performance could be observed. Later years brought some interesting characters into his life. One of them was a guide by the name of Arthur Leary. Several years after Wilfred had given up actual guiding, he was staying at Art's camp near Wolf Creek Spring Hole. Many times there we watched him go through his performance of peeling an egg. Art seldom boiled eggs, for fried eggs on pancakes were one of his special breakfasts. While I was helping Art wash the breakfast dishes one morning, he said, "Tomorrow morning I'll put an egg in hot water and then take it right out and we will see how good Wilfred is at this."

The next morning Wilfred must have suspected what was up, for he used extra precaution in starting his egg peeling. The laugh was on Art. Wilfred soon had the egg lying on his plate with only the skin on it, so soft it was almost as flat as a pancake. Not a drop leaked out. Wilfred looked at Art and said with a smile, "My lan, Harter, dat's de first time I was ever served a one-second egg."

The river was good for paddling this trip, and the noon hour found us at Camp Uncle Sam. Uncle Steve Ward was there and invited us for a nice trout dinner, which we quickly accepted. We arrived at Camp Betsy just in time for supper. The wonderful smell of frying potatoes greeted us as we toted our load of provisions to the kitchen.

In a few days the fly fishermen were bringing in many large trout. Everyone had all the speckled beauties he could eat. The sportsmen who stayed at Wilfred's camp, as well as at others on the river, never kept any more trout than the number they could eat in one day. Along about the middle of July the sports decided not to bring into camp any trout under sixteen inches in length from this time on until the end of the season. No trout under this length were eaten, and no one went without plenty of trout to eat. It soon became a disgrace for anyone on the river that summer to be seen with a trout under the self-imposed length just mentioned. It seemed that every day the trout would bite, rain or shine, hot or cold, and with any kind of weird combination of bait or lure. Never in the history of the Oswegatchie was the fishing so good. What was the reason? Only one thing, people said. The log booms allowing the passage of boats had created a great cool hiding place four miles long, and the cold water running from one spring hole downstream to the next spring hole was kept cool. Some guides claimed the bugs and worms from the bark on the logs made feed for the trout, but examination of trout stomachs did not support this theory. The guides' feelings toward the log jobbers changed to a much better mood.

The old-time guides, however, and a few of the natives knew this was just a peak of the fishing cycle in the Oswegatchie. Wilfred told me during one of our trips to High Falls that sometimes nature made a wonderful fishing hole and then destroyed it. When we came to a large, sandy, shallow spot in the river, he told me that this spot used to be called the Royal Fish Hole and was a large, fine, cool place where many big trout were taken. He then went on to explain how nature had washed the dirt away from the roots of a large tree upstream from this spot and the tree had fallen into the river. During high water sand had sifted through the branches and gradually filled the fishing hole until it was completely destroyed. He went on to state that such a happening was nothing to what men can do to wreck the woods and the natural beauty of this fine country.

I noticed that Wilfred felt rather gloomy. Soon he told me he had just discovered that some of the jobbers had dynamited some rocks out of the channel at Round Hill Rapids. This left a rough and jagged bottom dangerous for canoes and other boats and also spoiled the fishing at that spot. Once dynamited, a trout hole is no longer any good at all. He also told me that a section of Ross Rapids had suffered the same fate.

Fishing at High Falls was better than ever when the logs were in the river in spite of all the dire predictions that the trout would stay under the logs and not go to the falls. The guides surely had their nerves and patience sorely tried more than ever before, for they had to spend a lot of time extricating the fishermen's flies from logs and alders on shore as well as from the rocks. But there was lots of fun and good times which made up for the hard, exasperating work.

Smoke was getting thicker by the latter part of August and a few of the small fires got larger. The sportsmen began to move out of the woods. All of the mills were shut down, for the mill men joined the lumbermen in fighting fires. Many fires started in different sections of the company property, so only a few men were available to fight some of them. The sparks carried by the wind quickly spread the fires through the slashes left by the lumbermen. Wanakena village was practically surrounded by fire by September. The smoke was stifling. Flames neared the railroad from Wanakena to Benson Mines at the halfway water hole. They seared the paint on the coaches, which were thoroughly doused at the water hole. The section gang fought the fires at this point, trying to keep the trestles and ties from burning.

Thousands of dollars' worth of damage was done to the forests, but luckily the town, the mills, and the lumberyards were saved from the raging flames. When the fire reached virgin timber, the green trees allowed it to burn just a few rods into the forest and then it gradually died out. Hundreds of acres smoldered for weeks after the rain had put out the visible fire. The dry duff continued to burn and every once in a while would break out in flame. This continued late into the fall until plenty of rain and snow arrived.[12] In many places the duff was entirely burned up and only bare rocks remained of what once was a mighty forest.

Man's efforts to stop a roaring forest fire are so pitiful that it seems useless to describe some of the methods tried. To the inexperienced in woodcraft I might mention that seldom do large areas of virgin forest burn up until some stupid lumberman cuts it down. In the mad scramble for the dollar obtained in ruining the forest, a little time spent lopping off the tops and limbs and making them lie flat on the ground where they would soon decay would be well rewarded, but the greed of people for the almighty dollar overshadows the well-being of future generations. There is now a law which is supposed to make the jobber lop the tops, but it is poorly enforced.

When I arrived in my home town two weeks after school had started, my eyes were still swollen and red from so much smoke. I enjoyed telling the boys of my escape from the terrible Adirondack forest fires. But that wasn't all I had to tell them after my second summer in the woods. There was also the big fight.

7. THE BIG FIGHT

Many interesting things happened in the area. One of the highlights was Bob Fitzsimmons' fight with Jim Paul, the hero of the North Woods lumber camps, in a boxing match at Benson Mines, September 21, 1908. By that date I should have been in school back home in Ellicottville, but two things kept me in Wanakena late that year. One was the forest fires that continued into a dry September. The other was the scheduled coming of Robert Prometheus Fitzsimmons to the Ellsworth Hotel. No boy of thirteen could miss either of those events. They were the best part of my education that year.

As boxers go, Bob was already an old man in 1908. But at forty-six he was still going strong. He had lost the light-heavyweight and the heavyweight championships to younger men, but he was still the middleweight champion of the world. He never lost this title in his thirty years of professional boxing.

For several days before his appearance at Benson Mines, we had been reading about the great man in the *Watertown Daily Times*. He was at the Orpheum Theatre in Watertown on a vaudeville circuit, for Bob was an actor too. He and his wife were appearing in a little play called "A Man's a Man for A' That," which was based on a story of his life as a fighter. Bob also put on a bag punching act, and his wife sang. According to the *Times* reporter, her "splendid voice won many encores," and she was "one of the most elegantly dressed women ever seen on the stage in this city . . . adorned with a fortune in precious stones." Benson Mines and Wanakena hadn't seen much elegance or many precious stones, so we were looking forward to cheering Mrs. Fitz as well as her famous husband.

The *Watertown Daily Times* paid more attention to our area in 1908 than it did in most years, and the clippings can be found in family albums in Wanakena. I guess the *Times* reporter was about as excited as I was over the fight at Benson Mines, but he knew he was going to have to write it up and I didn't. Today I can't sort out the lefts from the rights or remember just when Mr. Fitz unpacked the famous solar plexus punch he had invented in his fight with Jim Corbett in 1897, when he knocked out an Irishman on St. Patrick's Day and won the world's heavyweight championship. So here is the story mostly in the words of the newspaper.

The *Times* reporter was more impressed than I was by the crowd. He said that it was an odd crowd that came to the fight, for the North Country was composed of all kinds of people. There was everybody from blanket-coated Canadian lumberjacks to miners who had knocked off early to come to Spain's and talk over the coming fight of their boys. By the time Ralph Barter, who was to do the scientific sparring, had arrived, the hotel office and barroom was crowded until there was hardly breathing space left for Fitz to welcome Ralph, which gave the crowd their first glimpse of the famous fighter. There was jabbering in French and English, and most people were surprised that Fitz wasn't a bigger man. When Jim Paul arrived with his supporters, most of the crowd gathered around him in front of the hotel.

Paul weighed as much as Fitz, which was about 165 pounds, but he was not as tall nor did he have the old man's reach. Paul said, "I comes har to fight. I don't know how hard he hit. Let him knocka me down. I fighting lumberjack." He went into the ring with the instructions only to go at Fitz for all he was worth, and he didn't really know whether the other fighter was out to do him or not.

The bouts were put on in the hotel hall, which was a large room that accommodated most of the crowd. The smoke of the burning forests had come in through the open windows of the hall, and this affected both Fitz and Barter. After an hour or two of moving pictures Barter stepped forth and announced the first bout between Jim Paul and Fitzsimmons. The old man with the broad shoulders made the woodsman look small, at least from the hips up. Fitz was a little knock-kneed and his legs were so thin that he wore thick knee-length underwear to cover them up. People called him "a cannonball on a pair of pipe stems." Maybe it was the trade of blacksmith he had learned as a boy in New Zealand that gave him such a figure. One of his many nicknames was the Village Blacksmith. While in Watertown, he went to a blacksmith's shop and forged horseshoes to give to the friends he made in the city.

52

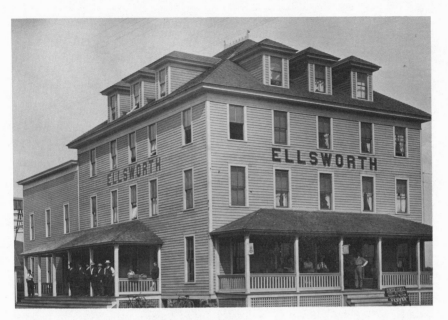

ELLSWORTH HOTEL AT BENSON MINES
Here Bob Fitzsimmons fought Jim Paul in 1908. *(Courtesy Carrie Spain)*

Referee Bart Lyman introduced the fighters. Mrs. Fitz held the watch and Barter's brother Gilbert, of Johnstown, New York, pulled the bell at the call of time.

Fitz stood away and Paul, after fiddling around a bit, came at him. The crowd had been warned not to make remarks, but they couldn't keep down their feelings when their man landed on the blacksmith's ribs. It didn't seem to bother Fitz and he countered lightly. Then Paul began the tactics which had won him victory in the battles in lumber camps. He leaped up and down like a grasshopper and tried to close in on the pugilist. This made it easy for Fitz, and on the breakaway he managed to rock Paul with some hooks to the head. Rough and tumble didn't do in prize fighting, the lumberjack found, so he tried to get in and away under Bob's apparently loose guard. He did better at this, and the first round went to Paul.

In the second round Fitz had warmed up and went after the log driver. He knocked Paul down. Paul quickly recovered, but it brought the crowd to their feet and Lyman had difficulty getting them back on their chairs. Fitz continued to force matters and kept Paul on the run, which gave the crowd good entertainment. He worked his famous shift considerably. Paul seemed to be without much defense against it except to back away as fast as he could.

Fitz had promised to give more than just a tapping match. In the final part of the round, after waiting for Paul, he reached over and put his left in the lumberman's stomach. Paul's hands dropped and Fitz had to grab him and shake him to keep him from going down. After the match Fitz said, "His stomach was right up against his heart, and it would have been a shame to give so game a fighter the finisher right then." When Paul had somewhat recovered, Fitz put a couple to the head and the bout ended. Paul wasn't sure of the way out and had trouble finding his corner. First he started to sit down on Mrs. Fitzsimmons' lap. Then someone turned him around, and after shaking hands with Fitz and being assured that it was all over, he was able to find his corner.

Fitz wasn't excited by the episode with Paul and immediately took on Barter. This go was way ahead of what had been scheduled as a fight with Paul. Barter had skill, weight, and experience and fought very evenly with Fitz. They pounded each other hard on the head, but there seemed to be an understanding that Fitz didn't have to protect his solar plexus. Once Ralph knocked Fitz down and they rolled on the floor in a clinch. It was real sport for both of them. They hit away at full speed, good heavy punches, but landing at nonvital points. It was a good exhibition of heavy hitting. There was no holding off and just a succession of jabs, hooks, and swings all the time until the gong sounded.

With the exception of the time Barter took off his coat one day at Carthage and worked out with Paul, it was the first time Paul had really been beaten. He had traveled around the lumber camps of the North Woods where it was his custom to throw his hat in front of the main shack and call the best man in the camp to come out and fight him. He had always won these fights. He came to be known as the fighting lumberjack and in the woods was acknowledged as a man invincible with his fists. It was a surprise for his friends to see him beaten so easily by Fitz, but then he had never faced a man who was both a boxer and a fighter. Paul's friends stood around for long hours discussing the match and woefully admitting that the North Woods hadn't developed a champion as they thought. Old Fitz had thoroughly sold himself to all who saw his exhibition.

Previous to the fight Sam Spain, the proprietor of the Ellsworth Hotel, feared that he would have trouble with Sheriff Hyland of Canton, for the sheriff had phoned Spain and told him the whole affair had to be conducted within the law. That was why Mr. Spain admitted everyone free for the fights after the moving pictures and the Fitzsimmons vaudeville sketch. No decision was given by the referee, so there wasn't any trouble with the authorities.

Next to the boxing the thing that pleased the crowd the most was the singing Mrs. Fitzsimmons did. The hotel lacked props and scenes for the sketch, but Promoter Spain was not lacking in invention, for the telephone was ripped off the wall for a prop and some of his best furniture from the parlor was used on the stage. When Fitz gave his curtain speech, he showed his originality and disproved the story that he only knew one speech which had been written for him by a New York newspaperman. His speech had personality, and when he came to the part where he said, "If my hands had remained unbroken, I would have written an even more enduring page in the history of pugilism than I have," the audience cheered. This was a reference to the 1902 fight in which Fitz broke all the knuckles of his right hand against James Jeffries' jaw.

In the morning, while Fitz was waiting for the train, he sat on the porch and told stories of his experiences to the interested people gathered there with him. He said, "I fought three bare fist fights with men before I was fifteen. In all my thirty years of fighting, in which I have engaged in 369 battles, I never trained until I came to America about twenty years ago. Why, when I was matched to fight the champion of Queensland or New South Wales out home, I would never even look at the bills. I would leave the blacksmith shop, run home to supper, and then make for the ringside. One fellow, an Englishman, came to my dressing room and told me how he was in no condition, so he wanted me to set to at first and then at the end he would do what he could for himself. The first thing that fellow did was to wallop me in the stomach, and I felt just like Jim Paul did last night when I reached on to his abdomen. I stayed the round and in the second fought even. In the third he got it so hard that he would not come for the next round, which I figured would be the last. When I fought Corbett . . ." and then the Wanakena Special tooted for the station and Bob, hearing Mrs. Fitz calling through the fog, made off for the station.

Jim Paul had a return bout with Fitzsimmons at the fair ground in Watertown a few days later. Afterwards he summed up the two fights accurately, "De more I heet, de more I mees." It was a hard thing for the lumberjacks to see their man lose, even if it was to a world champion.

55

8. THE GENERAL STORE AND THE HOTEL

I guess eating was one of the greatest pleasures of my youth as well as of the rest of my life. When red raspberries were ripe, I picked several quarts a day. Some went into pies and the remainder were canned by my grandmother. I raved about how good Grandmother's pies were until she said I should spend more time berrying so she could put up a few quarts for me to take home to use in pies during the winter. I carried out her suggestion very gladly. When the huckleberries were ripe, I picked some of them also for Grandmother to can for me. My grandfather and I had fresh huckleberries in bread and milk for supper during the season. If you have never tried this combination, you should do so at the first chance.

There was a clerk in the Rich and Andrews Store who used to give me bits of cheese, pickles, olives, and crackers whenever pangs of hunger were getting the best of me between meals. In this store you could buy almost anything you wanted, and if they didn't have it you could order from a catalogue. In a few days it was in the store.

In the basement were fifty-gallon barrels of vinegar, salt pork, sour pickles, sweet pickles, olives (large and small), molasses, corned beef, and many other liquid and brine-prepared staples. The main floor contained many barrels of cookies, crackers, sugar, and oatmeal. Large tin-foil-lined chests of tea and plenty of cheeses, tubs of butter, lard, and other items were also found here. The clerks were so adept at scooping or cutting amounts you ordered that a set of scales seemed almost unnecessary. The patent medicines and drug department consisted of hundreds of bottles. The store cat always slept among them and yet never tipped any over. At the front of the store was a large rack displaying shoes from the latest style of button shoe to the lumberjack's calked boots. Only one shoe of each kind was shown, never a pair, and occasionally a French Canadian would be seen walking around town with two different kinds of shoes on. Some of the Canucks helped themselves to the sample shoes just as to a cracker out of the barrel and finally had to be told the shoes were not samples to take home.

56

A long nicely varnished counter extended part way down the left side as you entered the store. The top was marked off in yards and fractions of a yard with little round-headed brass nails so it was convenient to measure the yard goods. This counter was the only clear spot in the whole store, and sometimes the train crew and some of the other workers would sit on it in their dirty overalls. One of the clerks patiently wired all the nails together underneath the counter where they stuck through and then hooked up a good strong spark coil which could be operated by a switch on the opposite side of the room. One day when six or seven of the town's prize sitters were comfortably seated on the counter, the switch was thrown. Several of the women customers were bowled over in the rush. From that day on, the dress goods counter was as clean as a whistle.

Sometime during the cold hard winter the dry goods salesman would arrive with his twenty large trunks full of sample goods, and of course the word of his coming was passed around. His arrival was a big time for all and especially for the ladies. A temporary counter was placed down the center of the store where the salesman could lay out his wares. The store customers would look at the display and tell the clerks what they wanted to buy. These goods were left out for three to five days so that the lumberjacks and other workers from the surrounding camps could all have a chance to order what they wanted. It was quite a sight to see the salesman pack all those samples away in his specially built

RICH AND ANDREWS GENERAL STORE ABOUT 1908
"You could buy almost anything you wanted."

trunks. The commission he got from the goods which were ordered justified the twenty-five-cent cigar he smoked as a sort of celebration.

The top floor of the store was the clothing department. It was well stocked with an assortment from the latest style of men's suits to blankets and mattresses. The remnant counter was well patronized, and many school kids wore snow suits of assorted colors. Some of the heavy items sold at the store were wagons, sleighs, harnesses, oats, hay, coal, feed, ice, and stoves. The store carried about sixty thousand dollars' worth of stock. There was a large porch built across the front end, and a covered platform ran its entire length. Beside the platform ran the railroad siding.

The Cranberry Lake Railroad, owned by the Rich Lumber Company, was only six miles in length. In those days presidents of railroads exchanged passes. The president of the Cranberry Lake Railroad sent for a pass on a Southern line of considerable mileage. His request was answered by, "We do not exchange passes with such small railroads." The Cranberry Railroad president sent the reply, "Our railroad may not be as long as yours, but it is just as wide." In a short while he received an annual pass from the Southern road.

The railroad brought many visitors to Wanakena. There were not only the sportsmen who hired guides to take them up the river or out on the big lake, but also the sitters on the hotel veranda. The general store was not alone in doing a large volume of business. The Hotel Wanakena, which the Rich Lumber Company began to build in 1902, became popular with New York City guests. For several years, during the summer season, a sleeper left Grand Central Terminal for Wanakena via Utica and Carthage every Friday night. The Cranberry Lake Railroad drew this sleeper into the woods from Benson Mines to Wanakena, and it was parked on the siding by the general store until Sunday afternoon, when it left for its return trip.

A water mail route for summer months was established by the Post Office Department and still operates at this writing. While the Cranberry Lake Railroad was still operating, most of the mail for the cottages and hotels around the lake was picked up in Wanakena. Later the village of Cranberry Lake became the principal distribution center when the Grass River Railroad gave that village a connection with the Mohawk and Malone at Childwold. The first of the mail boats that I knew was the *Helen,* propelled by steam. It received its mail, express, and passengers from the train which arrived at Wanakena every day around noon. Later a large boat run by a gasoline engine, the first of its

FRONT STREET AND THE HOTEL WANAKENA ABOUT 1908
The hotel is in the background. Note the wooden sidewalk.
(Courtesy George McAlister)

kind on the lake, replaced the old *Helen,* which kept up its usefulness by towing logs and rafts of lumber on the lake. The new boat, the *Wanakena,* was faster and much larger, cutting mail delivery time down considerably and having a capacity of a hundred people. The pilot was George Shamp and the purser Stanley Locke. Besides the daily mail delivery and passenger service, there was an excursion trip on Sunday. Riding the mail boat became a popular pastime.

These good communications and the fact that the forest, the lake, and the river were just off the front veranda gave the Hotel Wanakena a strong appeal to city people who liked to sit and sniff the piney, balsamy air. The hotel made the most of its advantages. Billy Bean, who operated it till the Rich Lumber Company moved out, knew how to make people feel at home. O. G. Rich, the proprietor who succeeded Bean, was not such a popular host but brought Madison Avenue advertising into the woods. Here is a sample from the little booklet, accompanied by twelve illustrations, which he put out on the Hotel Wanakena, "a famous hostelry of the North Woods, the gateway to the beautiful Cranberry Lake Region":

59

"FOR pleasure, health, rest, and recreation, for scenes and surroundings that charm the eye, soothe the mind, and quiet the nerves—for blood-building, balsam-laden air to fill the lungs, and the purest of mountain spring water to flush the system—in short, for a perfect pleasure-ground, a health rebuilding paradise—there is none to equal *The Adirondacks.*

"HERE, just a step, as it were, off the main line of railroad travel between the west and the east, is New York State's playground, where mountain, river, lake, and forest combine to delight the vacationist or the health seeker. Here is game for the hunter, trout for the fisherman. Here is boating, canoeing, sailing, tramping over trails worn a hundred years ago by the soft-footed moccasin of the red man.

"AND right in the heart of this wonderful region, easily accessible yet seemingly far distant from civilization as exemplified by noisy paved streets and skyscraper buildings, is Beautiful Wanakena.

"SITUATED picturesquely on the bank of the Oswegatchie River but a little way from where it flows into Cranberry Lake is the Inn of the North Woods, known to some as Hotel Wanakena.

"THIS popular hostelry stands for practically all of the conveniences of the great modern city hotel, transported far into the primeval forest, where one can go out, catch his trout, and bring it in to be fried for his breakfast.

"IN the Adirondacks one could sleep refreshingly on the mossy side of a pine plank. He would be loath therefore to rise from The Wanakena's comfortable beds were it not for the desire to get the inspiring view from his own windows of green forest and sturdy mountain, of a lovely landscape inlaid with glistening river and shimmering lake; and one hurries outdoors to breathe in, again and again, all his lungs will hold of the purest, sweetest, cleanest, ozone-filled air, a dozen whiffs of which at daybreak will send the blood jumping merrily through one's veins and make him glad just to be living.

"THEN after breakfast eaten with zest born of an appetite aroused, the day's program is looked forward to with enthusiasm. Maybe, it's a canoe or boating trip to the coves and inlets of Cranberry, or a motorboat trip around this largest and one of the most picturesque of Adirondack lakes.

"THEN there is fishing, hunting in season, bowling, billiards, swimming, baseball, tennis, and dancing. Oh, time never hangs heavy at Wanakena! And should the day be rainy, or the evening cool, the large, old, open fireplaces with their blazing logs add much to indoor pleasure and comfort.

"THE dining rooms at the Wanakena are unusually light, commodious, and pleasant. The linen and silver are nice, the service quiet and well-trained, and the menu excellent. In fact, the Wanakena is a hotel where, having enjoyed its hospitality once, you look forward to returning again and again, and you tell your friends of the pleasure of your vacation here, of the reasonable rates, the large airy rooms, and the home-like comforts and surroundings. Steam heat, electric lights, private baths, rooms en suite, if desired, all help to make your visit to Hotel Wanakena a happy one. . . .

"FOR those who prefer more quiet seclusion a number of charming cottages prettily situated adjacent to the hotel, well furnished and with electric lights, running water, baths, etc., may be rented at reasonable rates.

"FROM June 1st to October 1st connections will be made with all trains. People with tubercular trouble are requested not to apply for accommodations. For terms and other information, address

HOTEL WANAKENA
O. G. Rich, Proprietor, Wanakena, New York."

In spite of their merrily jumping blood, many patrons of the hotel preferred just to sit. The sitters on the railroad platform at the general store never forgot the sitters on the hotel veranda. I guess they felt a kind of rivalry over who could sit longest. One day when the platform sitters were asked to lend a hand to a neighbor, they were thinking as usual about the veranda sitters. So it came natural to them to pass the request on to the hotel veranda.

The man who made the request was a newcomer to Wanakena named Mr. Phillips. He and his wife were both in their seventies. They had given up their farm near Lowville, New York, because the work load was getting to be too much of a burden. Their son-in-law, Bert Dobson, gave them a piece of land on the outskirts of Wanakena bor-

61

HOTEL WANAKENA SEVERAL YEARS LATER
This photo shows the addition on the fore side. The hotel stood on high ground where sitters on the veranda enjoyed a good view over Inlet Flow and sniffed the balsam-scented air. *(Courtesy Pearl Morrison)*

dering the state land and built them a comfortable cottage. They were happy in their new home. They put a fence around their lot and built a small henhouse and a barn just large enough for a cow and a horse. They produced their own eggs and milk and on Sunday enjoyed a chicken dinner.

This fine old couple never asked for relief or other financial help. Mrs. Phillips took in washing and ironing, though she had no washing machine or electric iron. Her flatirons were heated on a wood stove, for which her husband cut the fuel. He also cut grass around the village for his cow and horse and earned a little money by small carting jobs with his horse and wagon.

One morning when there were sitters on the platform at the general store, Mr. Phillips stopped in front of them and asked if they knew of anyone he could get to turn his grindstone. His scythe was getting too dull to sharpen with a whetstone. One of the platform wits spoke up: "You go up to the hotel and you will find several men sitting in comfortable rocking chairs on the front porch. Ask if one of them will turn your grindstone."

Mr. Phillips went to the hotel as directed and asked, "Would one of you men come over to my house and turn the grindstone so I can sharpen my scythe?" After a short silence a handsome white-haired old gentleman said, "I'll be glad to help you. I haven't turned a grindstone since I was a boy."

They soon had a fine edge on the scythe. Then the hotel guest asked, "Don't you have an ax or some other tool that needs an edge?" An ax, some chisels, and some kitchen knives got the same treatment. Then Mrs. Phillips emerged from the side door and said, "Mister, please come in and have a home cooked meal with us." Seeing that the invitation was sincere, the hotel guest accepted. Later he told the old couple that he hadn't had a meal like that since those his mother used to make when he was a boy.

A few days later when the platform sitters were working at their favorite profession, Mr. Phillips happened to pass by. With a grin the wit asked how he had made out at the hotel. "A man came," said Mr. Phillips gravely, "and we sharpened all my tools. Then he had dinner with us." It was a whole hour before the platform sitters got their usual cockiness back.

9. FISHING AND A RIDE ON THE MAIL BOAT

Winter and spring soon passed, and I was again a very excited passenger getting off the train at Benson Mines. I was anxious to see the damage done by the forest fires. The first words I heard were, "By de gee whiz, how is de kid?" My friend Wilfred was at the station to meet a fishing party that was going to the Inlet House for some rapids fishing.

There were four kinds of trout fishing during the season. Early flow, lake, rapids, and upriver they were called. As soon as the ice went out of the lake, flow trout started to bite around the old docks and on the rocky shoals. Bait fishing was about all that would produce trout at this time. Trolling was also popular, and some large ones were hooked in this way. Fly fishing was not good at this time of year. When the water warmed up, chubs, red fins, and bullheads started to bite, and the trout began going up the Rapids, where they remained for a while before going on up to the spring holes and High Falls. Some trout remained in the spring holes around the Flow and the lake, and many headed for Brandy Brook Flow on the eastern shore of Cranberry Lake. This place became very famous for its fishing.

About four weeks of extremely good fishing was enjoyed on the Rapids each spring. Flies, spinners, worms, and minnows all caught their share on the Rapids, and many dollars' worth of tackle was lost trying to save a big trout in the swift white water. Toward the latter part of May the big trout began to reach High Falls, and the famous trout fly stream was ready for the experts to try their luck. A few sportsmen came for all the different kinds of fishing, but of course the real dyed-in-the-wool fly fishermen never would use worms. Therefore they didn't care for the early flow and lake fishing.

Up until 1920, even in July and August a couple of days of fair fishing on the Rapids followed a rain heavy enough to raise the river. Large trout were taken here by the natives who knew the habits of the big fish and how to get them to bite. Slowly the inroads of civilization upon this spot began. An automobile had reached Benson Mines. Soon many trout could be taken out. Fishermen would not have to stop catching them when they had enough for immediate use. People were beginning to get restless in their eagerness to reach the woods quickly. There was still no need for immediate worry because the roads were passable only during a short dry summer, and hardly anyone in those days dreamed of good roads ever reaching this section.

In the summer of 1909 very few logs were left in the river, and by August they were entirely cleaned out. The jack works was removed and the spur from the main log railroad was taken up. The fish catching had dropped off considerably but was still all anyone could reasonably desire. This year Wilfred introduced me to a very famous guide, Bert Dobson, the proprietor of Dobson's Camps at High Falls, where about forty guests could be accommodated. Many people came there to rest, read, write, fish, or just loaf, and it was a jolly group one would meet at the camp. "Wilfred," Bert stuttered, "I have a s-s-sport here with two thousand dollars' worth of fishing tackle. Can't catch a trout over a pound, is always grumbling about poor fishing, and has s-s-several of the new guests almost believing him."

Soon the man just described came into the main camp where we were and where several other guests were sitting playing cards or reading. This sportsman seemed to be greatly peeved over his poor results during the morning of fishing and said to Bert, "There isn't a large trout in this damn river. I'm going someplace where there is." Bert replied,

64

A GOOD CATCH
  Bert Dobson nets a brook trout hooked by his party at Crooked Rapids.
  (Courtesy Marion Sawyer)

"You don't know how to catch them," whereupon the sport got upset and said, "I'll bet you a drink for everyone at this camp you can't catch a fish over a pound in the next hour." "I'll take that bet," Bert replied.

Bert got his flyrod and everyone followed him down to the pool at the foot of the falls except the man who made the bet with him. Bert had the reputation of being able to catch large trout when no one else was able to. After a few casts he dropped the fly over his favorite spot and in a second had hooked a large trout. He played it carefully while someone ran up to the camp to bring the news to the sport, who came running down and whose face turned red when he saw Bert leading the big trout around in the pool. There was a large audience as Bert guided the three-pounder into his net. Wetting his hands well, he removed the fly from the trout's lip. As the sport reached for the beautiful big fish, Bert let it slip back into the water and said, "There, God damn it, now catch it yourself." Everyone gave the fellow the horse laugh and took an expensive drink because he was known as a cheap sort of guy. This episode cured all complaints of poor fishing for that summer.

We were invited to stay for dinner. The memory of Mrs. Dobson's wonderful fresh raspberry pie will always stay in my mind. Many guests

65

came to the Dobson camps year after year because of the tasty meals, or perhaps the restful roar of the falls, or the smell of the great white pines that stood towering into the skies around the camps. It would be hard to imagine a better place for a restful and happy vacation.

After dinner Wilfred and I started to walk to Wanakena by a new route (for me) which went across the Plains and along Glasby Brook, joined the Cat Mountain Trail, and then went to Dead Creek Flow, where the log train had just received its last carload of logs from the Jack Works for that day. We got on the end of the rear car and rode the remaining two and a half miles to Wanakena.

On a gorgeous Adirondack morning in August the genial proprietor of the Hotel Wanakena suggested that we take a ride around Cranberry Lake with the mailman as he made his daily trip delivering mail to the hotels and cottages. Leaving Wanakena, we twisted through and by the dead trees lining the channel of Inlet Flow and dodged the many stumps just under water. The pilot knew where they all were, for, as he said, he had hit them often enough.

About four miles down the Flow, where the river enters Dead Creek Flow, is a spot rightfully named the Hawk's Nest. The flooding of the land here made a weird and alluring sight. Both banks had been covered with virgin timber. After the dam was built, some of the higher land was converted into little islands on which a few trees survived. The trees on the drowned land died and in time turned into thickly clustered gaunt specters. Many of these white pines, hemlocks, and spruces were cut, for, being dead and dry, they were easy to float. They were used for making docks and even sawed up for lumber. Some were cut during the winter when the Flow was frozen over. If the lake was high before it iced over and the snow was deep, the stumps were left quite high above normal water level; others were considerably lower. Some of the guides used to explain to their parties that the high ones were cut by Paul Bunyan the year he had a backache and couldn't bend over. In all cases the branches and tops were left to float around in the spring flood. In some places it was difficult even to row a skiff without hitting logs, stumps, or tangled driftwood. The old channel had to be marked with suitable markers so that power boats could safely navigate this area.

The floating debris moved around and often came to rest over spring holes and in cool coves where big trout could hide and thrive. The fishing was generally good all summer here because of the floating shelter. Hundreds of big speckled beauties made their home underneath tangled treetops until the time in the fall when nature called them to their spawning beds many miles above the Rapids. Nature lovers and game club members of those days tried to maintain this natural environment to promote the growth and propagation of the trout. The beautiful fish had not as yet met the conservation politicians and were therefore enjoying the life nature planned for them.

Rounding the Hawk's Nest, we headed into Dead Creek Flow. To both the right and left we could see hundreds of acres of virgin forest.[13] We ran toward shore for about a mile on an easterly course and then cut diagonally across to the opposite shore to a two-storied log camp called Tramps Retreat, which was owned by a nature lover, a Mr. Ames Howlett. This camp (destroyed by lightning and fire in 1957) was surrounded by virgin forest. After landing at a large dock, we were invited in to see the trophies Mr. Howlett had collected in his travels about the Adirondacks and other parts of the world. The main room of the camp was cheerfully pouring forth hospitality with warmth from a mammoth stone fireplace. The floor of the upper story was supported by large hand-hewed square timbers which were so stately looking in their duties that it seemed as if they wanted to tell you about the master of the broad ax who had carved them from the forest. Steel traps hung in a continuous band all around the room and ranged from tiny mouse catchers to a large blacksmith-made bear trap. They formed a very interesting border. Each and every one had notches filed on the springs which recalled many exciting and thrilling tales to the owner. What pleasure this fine old man had experienced! What fun it must have been for him to tell his adventures to his grandchildren in front of this glowing fireplace! Animal heads and stuffed birds of all kinds were mounted around the room. We thanked our host for the pleasant half hour and went on our way.

After leaving Tramps Retreat, we saw on our port side thousands of tamarack poles sticking up out of water, for this had been a tamarack swamp before the lake level had been raised by the dam. It is now called the Hopyard. On our port side appeared Joe Indian Island, which is the largest island in Cranberry Lake though it is less than three-quarters of a mile long and one-quarter wide. On our starboard side a pretty point came into view, and we saw a large building on it which our pilot told us was the Deremo Hotel. For a long time it was famous for its Saturday night square dances. Wanakena people used to load onto a large lumber scow and be towed to these dances, where everyone had a wonderful time.

As we passed the point, we noticed another heavily wooded island on our port side called Buck Island, which was owned by a noted wild-woods lover, Judge Irving Vann of Syracuse. After passing the island, we headed in a southeasterly direction until we came to one of the most popular hotels on the lake, Nunn's Inn. This was located at the southern end of the main lake, which is called "the head of the lake" because it is flanked by two important feeders, Six Mile Creek and Chair Rock Creek, and perhaps because it is opposite the outlet at the north end. We spent quite a little time at this place. Some of the passengers on the boat who had been on this trip before decided to stay here for one of Nunn's famous dinners and catch the boat on its return trip.

I visited with one of the hotel guests who had returned regularly for many summers. He told of a friend of his who always caught more large trout than any of the other guests. The reason for this was that he had found a good spot where the fish always seemed to bite. He never told anyone about it but always fished alone there. One night it was rumored at the bar that this fisherman was using dynamite. The story grew and traveled till it finally reached the ears of the local game warden. One day he appeared at the hotel disguised in sportsman clothes and then had the proprietor point out the large trout catcher. The game warden struck up an acquaintance with the fisherman and then after a few beers asked if he could go fishing with him that evening. After a few more beers the fisherman agreed. They started out rowing about dusk. When they got behind a point of land, the fisherman stopped rowing and told the warden that here was where they were going to get some big ones.

The warden, sitting in the stern of the boat, started to rig up his equipment. The fisherman reached into a bag, pulled out a stick of dynamite, lit the fuse, and said, "Now you will have a chance to fish the easy way," as he tossed the dynamite to the game warden and added, "Throw it right in back of you as far as you can." The warden caught it and threw it right back. The fisherman threw it again to the warden and hollered, "Throw it!" It made one more round trip till the warden decided it was time to get rid of it and threw it as far as he could. Nothing happened. The fisherman said that he guessed the caps weren't any good and that they would have to try another one.

Thinking that he had enough evidence, the warden said he was cold and wanted to go back to the hotel. As soon as he had his feet safely planted on shore, he held open his coat to display his badge and said, "I'll take that bag of dynamite and also you." They walked up the path to the hotel, where all the guests were patiently waiting for the report on the fishing trip. The warden said to the guests, "Here is how your great fisherman has been having such good luck," and held up the bag of dynamite.

In the morning the warden took his prisoner to Cranberry Lake village. Most of the guests went along. They landed at the dock and went straight to the justice of the peace. There the fisherman was accused of a serious crime. The evidence was taken out of the bag and exhibited. But when the justice pulled out one of the fuses, he found that the stick was loaded with wet sawdust. Everyone laughed at the joke on the warden, and the case was dismissed.

As we left Nunn's, we could see several cottages on our right on a point of land. One of the buildings stood out conspicuously. Some men were on the porch drinking beer. We were told that this building was called the Pig's Ear and was operated by a Cranberry Lake guide named Will Mott. Our course now was along the east shore, past Sucker Brook, East, and Brandy Brook flows. At the foot of Bear Mountain was a place called Balderson's, a hotel which has contributed much to the memory of Cranberry Lake's many resorts. We continued on our way and soon arrived at Lone Pine Point, where John Howland entertained many summer people in his fine hotel. Nearby was another restful place called the Sunset Inn.

We soon arrived at the village of Cranberry Lake after passing pretty little Birch Island, a favorite place for shore dinners as there were no mosquitoes, punkies, or flies there to cause discomfort. Our pilot, George Shamp, tied up the *Wanakena* at the dock and took us to the White Birch Inn. We had a dinner unequaled in its luxurious tastiness, and yes, for dessert we had fresh wild raspberry pie and homemade ice cream. Yum! Yum! After dinner we visited the dam which controls the outlet. The operator of the gates, a Mr. Dean, told us that a few inches of the lake level were released each day according to the demands of the mills and power plants located downstream on the Oswegatchie River as it winds its way across St. Lawrence County to its mouth at Ogdensburg, where it flows into the St. Lawrence River.

On our return trip we crossed the foot of the lake and made a brief stop at the old Columbian Hotel, where many guests were enjoying the rest and comfort that these places far from the noise and dirt of civilization can give. We proceeded south along the west shore for a mile or so until the pilot said, "Those rocks sticking up on our port side are called Matilda Island. It is best to give them a wide berth in passing." We passed Gull Rock, disturbing the gulls that roost and raise their young there. We stopped again at Nunn's Inn and picked up the passengers we had left on the first stop there. Returning to Wanakena in the late afternoon, we found the dock covered with bathers. The diving board and the diving platform were in constant use as many enjoyed their daily swim and belly smackers. Our party all agreed that it was a day well spent and that it would not soon be forgotten.

One day late in August Wilfred and I paddled another load of provisions up to his camp. The amount of food eaten by his guests was amazing. Some of them hadn't eaten a meal in years without taking pills or a dose of medicine. A few days after they arrived at Wilfred's camp the pills and medicine served only as a subject of jest among the guests and the guides. The guests soon forgot to take their pills and were enjoying life as they hadn't done in years. Wondrous cures are wrought by nature when she is given half a chance.

One morning before the guests were awake Wilfred asked me to go to Carter's old campsite with him to borrow some coffee, for he had forgotten to buy any with his last order of provisions. As we paddled through Sugar Rapids, we could see a man fishing from the old railroad grade at Carter's Landing. When we reached the head of the rapids, Wilfred stopped paddling, took some night crawlers from my bait box, and put them in his pocket. When I asked him what he was doing, he said, "Wait, den you will see." When we landed the canoe, the man who had been fishing came down to meet us. Before we could even say "Good morning," he greeted Wilfred with, "Give me a chew of Warneke Brown." Instead of handing him the tobacco sack as he had done many times before and watched half his supply disappear, Wilfred reached in his pocket and pulled out a handful of Warneke Brown along with the night crawlers. The strong tobacco made them very lively, and they wiggled around like little snakes. The tobacco chewer on shore stood with his eyes almost popping out of his head as Wilfred picked the crawlers out of the tobacco. He tried to speak, with his mouth making up and down movements, until he finally managed to mumble, "Do you always keep your fish worms in your chewing tobacco?" Wilfred replied, "I do dat cause it keep it from getting too dry. I only smoke it, so it do not matter. When it is in de package, de worm stay on de bottom." The tobacco beggar turned and went back to his fishing. "Dere, by de gee," said Wilfred as we went on, "he is cure."

I went on to the camp and borrowed the coffee. When I got back, I found Wilfred had caught a nice three-pound trout at Carter's Spring Hole. His guests had fresh trout that flopped in the pan for breakfast. Some of the guests changed their vacations from July because it seemed

70

July went by so fast, but then they found August passed just as fast. So it went with my vacation. Summer slipped quickly by, and again it was time to leave the village and the way of life I had grown so comfortably into.

Wanakena had reached the height of its prosperity. Besides the Hotel Wanakena there was Conroy's Inn, a boarding house favored by lumberjacks. The village now boasted of a church, a reading room, a restaurant, a meat market, an ice cream parlor, a pool and billiard room, a dance hall, a bowling alley, a small bakery, a barber shop, a shoe repair shop, the general store, a telegraph office, and telephones. There was no bar, but I was too young to miss it. What a swell place to live and work! If only I would ever get old enough to leave school, here was the paradise I wanted to live in. The great fires had left hundreds of acres of black stumps and bare rocks, but by September 1909 much of this land had already started a rapid growth of berry bushes and fire and pin cherry trees. The deer and other animals liked to paw around on the burnt ground. In places where the fire had not been too hot, huckleberry and raspberry bushes were beginning to thrive. During the next nine months I thought of these things many times during school hours and on the long winter nights.

THE CENTER OF TOWN
The cross marks the back of the general store. Upstairs (circle) was a plumbing shop. On the siding is the weekend Pullman car from New York City. The building marked "2" is the post office, and "3" is the ice cream parlor and meat market. At the far left is Conroy's Inn.

(Courtesy Marion King)

10. TWO SHAMES: TIMBER THIEVES AND A MOTORBOAT AT HIGH FALLS

June finally came, and once again I climbed down from one of the old squealy coaches of the Carthage and Adirondack at Benson Mines. This night the crowd at the station had their backs to the train and were watching a lumberjack ride his "skidding" horse up the high steps to the Ellsworth Hotel bar. I arrived just in time to see horse and rider pull up to the bar and order a drink. Mr. Spain, the proprietor, was scared to death the horse would break through the floor, but it didn't. After receiving a beer for the rider and a lump of sugar for the horse, they left and all was normal again.

I didn't see my friend Wilfred around. Upon arriving at Wanakena, I learned he was taking a cure for drinking at some place where he had been sent willingly by one of the parties he guided every year. His drinking had begun to interfere with his guiding. After several weeks I heard that he would be coming back on a certain day.

The evening of that day many people were at the Benson Mines depot, for they all knew Wilfred and were anxious to see how he looked after taking the cure. When the train arrived, the passengers began to get off. As the last one hopped down, it was apparent that Wilfred was missing. The conductor, who knew practically all the people in the towns along his run, whispered to a couple of men he knew were Wilfred's friends. They got a disappointed look on their faces. They climbed aboard and in a minute appeared carrying a person who was very drunk. The crowd roared, for there was their hero smiling and happy. This was the first and only time in Wilfred's life he was not able to get on or off a train by himself.

He was taken to the hotel and put to bed to sleep it off. The next day he was around as usual and no worse for his experience. His benefactors were expected in a few days. Another guide had obtained a photo of his return to Benson Mines and planned to show it to them as a joke. A local photographer had been hired to take a picture of Wilfred cured and sober, but instead took one of Wilfred drunk and happy. There were always photographers, as well as peddlers of watches and jewelry, hanging around Benson Mines. There was always something to photograph and lumberjacks to buy jewelry.

I did not see Wilfred for almost a month, for when he was in town I was on a trip into the woods with the company scaler, Richard Hanley, who invited me to visit the different lumber camps with him while he was on his inspection trips. Mr. Hanley was a very large man and could walk all day and never get tired or slow his pace. It kept me running most of the time to keep up with him. He was one of the most friendly persons I ever met, and it was a pleasure to be with him. His duties in connection with the lumbering process were many. The boundary lines of the company tract bordered on land of the State Forest Preserve in several places, and it was a difficult task to keep the jobbers from going over the line a few feet for some likely looking timber. At one time, to pay their taxes, the people from whom the Rich Lumber Company had purchased a large tract had sold three hundred acres of forest land to the state. This parcel stuck out in a square chunk into the company property and of course could not be lumbered. Many a hunter became lost and confused in this parcel of big timber.

The scaling or measuring of the number of board feet of logs cut by the jobbers was slow work. We spent several days at each of the lumber camps while this was being done. The food served at the camps was good and plentiful. When you saw the amount of food eaten at each meal, you wondered how any jobber could pay the jacks and feed them also. Two large hills lie between Wanakena and the Plains five miles south. Between these hills in the valleys were two lumber camps called DeOtt's and DeShane's. Thousands of logs were cut from these locations and hauled down through the valleys to eventually reach the railroads that ran from the Dead Creek Flow Jack Works and the Plains to the sawmills in Wanakena. These are the camps I remember best of those I visited with Mr. Hanley.

When I returned to the village, I found Wilfred just about ready to leave for Inlet and another trip paddling up the river to his camp. He asked me to go with him. I didn't have to be asked twice. When we reached the Inlet House, Wilfred went to the bar for a beer. One of the men there said to the others, "Sorry Wilfred doesn't drink anymore since he took the cure, for I was just going to ask him to have one." Maybe they hadn't heard of the episode at his return, for they seemed surprised to hear him ask for a drink. When they asked him about his trip to take the cure, his story went something like this:

"When I arrive at de cure place, dey give me several big drink wid someting in dem to make me sick. After an hour dey give me a bigger drink wid more of de pisin, anudder hour and a bigger drink and more

A TYPICAL LUMBER CAMP
This was Jim Weston's lumber camp near Bassout Pond on the Abbott tract. Note the spruce bark roof.

(Courtesy Marion King)

pisin, but still I'm not sick and a happier buck never left de wood dan me. I heard one of de doctor say he never seen a beast he couldn't make sick on de drink dey give me. Tomorrow he would try anudder pisin. De next day was de same, and I was feeling like a king. So on to de next and de next. Den dey make me a waiter and I serve de drink to de oder gent. When one of dem got sick and couldn't drink his, I drink it for him. So for one mont I never spent such a swell time, and dey was glad to see me leave de place, for I was such a poor advertisement for dem."

When we arrived at Wilfred's camp that night, his guests were all excited. They had heard during the day that all the large white pines at High Falls were being cut down. The next morning Wilfred and I, with several of his guests, walked to High Falls. On the way we met several guests from the camps there who informed us that it was indeed true. The trees were lying on the ground like fallen soldiers. When we neared High Falls, we met two more men carrying packs, who with tears in their eyes said they were leaving this place forever. Many of the guests would have gladly given the lumber company the price of the trees if the pines had been left standing. These people went to the officials of

74

the company as soon as they arrived at Wanakena and told them what they thought of their meanness in cutting the High Falls pines, which they had promised to leave standing. The officials were horrified to hear what had happened and began looking at once for the jobber who had disobeyed their orders. He couldn't be found, knowing that he should keep out of sight. Some guides and guests threatened to chop off his legs or shoot him. No matter. The damage was done and never could be repaired. But if beating him would have brought back the trees, I for one would have gladly helped. It was found later that the cutting had been done out of spite because of hatred between two people.

The camps at High Falls were run by Bert Dobson, who advertised "rustic log cabins, comfortable rooms, good, plain, wholesome food, finest trout fishing and deer hunting to be found," all for $1.50 to $2 per day. "Some of the guests who have visited here are Irving Bacheller, Ernest Thompson Seton, Carmon Roberts, and other authors and naturalists. . . . Those who like to hunt with a camera can find ample opportunity to gratify their desires. On nearly any summer's evening, a short trip in a canoe will take the photographer to the places where deer

DOBSON'S CAMPS AT HIGH FALLS

This became a popular woods resort after the Rich Lumber Company surrendered the cabins to Bert Dobson. The sleeping quarters are at left, the cook shack at right.

(*Courtesy Marion Sawyer*)

come down to drink, and, so tame are these animals during the summer that the photographer will have no difficulty in securing several good pictures of them. Another interesting feature of this section of the country is a trip to the lumber camps, little villages by themselves deep in the heart of the forest, where there is an opportunity to see 'men with the bark on.' "

The cutting of the pines changed the prospects of Dobson's Camps. Business dropped off as faithful patrons who had loved the beauty as well as the isolation of the spot stopped coming. In time Bert Dobson gave up and left for another part of the Adirondacks. The company put a temporary caretaker at the camps to watch the contents and take care of the buildings.

When I got back to Wanakena, a boy friend of mine, Sternie Mac-Lane, whose father was an engineer on the Cranberry Lake Railroad, told me there were lots of huckleberries ripe at Flat Rock, three miles from town. He told me his father would let us ride down on the engine with him. We could fill our pails while the train was at the Mines and then return with it. We did this several times during August. My grandmother canned enough to last Grandpa all winter, and during the huckleberry season my grandfather's daily meal at night was bread and milk with the fresh berries. Try it some time if you are not too lazy to pick a few berries during your summer vacation in the Adirondacks. Don't expect to find too many of them, though, for they are getting shaded out by the rapid growth of trees and shrubs.

This summer also produced many quarts of wild raspberries to add to my grandmother's cellar of canned goods. I feel sorry for the boys with wives too lazy to put up a few home-canned berries for the winter and for those who have never tasted real homemade pie. During the long cold winter berry pies seemed to shorten the days until summer again rolled around.

After the forest fires and the Bob Fitzsimmons fight, *The Beast* was the greatest sensation of the years 1908 to 1910. *The Beast* was the forerunner of the most destructive device ever invented by man to ruin fishing on the upper Oswegatchie and other rivers. City people were impatient in their desire to rush to the woods quickly and easily. The fishermen of Wanakena were also anxious to reach, as rapidly and lazily as possible, the spring holes on the river above Inlet House. So they built a flat-bottomed boat with provision for a small propeller to turn and not extend below the bottom of the boat. The bottom had a tunnel in it to protect the propeller from logs and rocks. The idea of a power boat to run in low water among rocks and logs originated with one of the mechanics at the Rich Lumber Company's machine shop, a Mr. Burger. To turn the propeller, a one-cylinder, make-and-break engine was ordered from the Truscott Boat Manufacturing Company (which went out of business in 1920) of St. Joseph, Michigan.

When Wilfred first saw the contraption, he gave it the name of *The Beast*, which was later painted on its sides. During the summer of 1908 or 1909 the wildlife of High Falls saw, for the first time, a motorboat chug up to the pool below the falls in its haste to battle the life out of old Mother Nature.

A rudder was placed on the stern of *The Beast*, but it couldn't make the boat go around the sharp bends of the river and was often torn off by snags or rocks. So one man was assigned to ride in the bow with a pikepole and shove the nose around bends. Wilfred tried this kind of navigation several times but soon gave *The Beast* up except for occasional use in high water. After a year or two of fewer and fewer trips up the river, *The Beast* was tied up in a little cove below the landing at Inlet, where it gradually filled with water. During spring floods sand sifted into it and permanently sank it, never to float again. I often wondered if other people ever noticed it on their mad, flying trips up the river with their modern outboards designed to run successfully in shallow waters.

One day during the summer of 1938, when Wilfred and I were paddling down the river past the little cove, Wilfred said, "Dere is de old *Beast*." We could see the brass plate on the top of the engine shine as the sun hit it, though it was under a foot of water. "Some day," I said, "I am going to pull the old engine out and keep it for a souvenir."

Years later, in the summer of 1964, I was talking over my shortwave transmitter to Wesley Hammond of Leicester, New York, and told him about *The Beast*. His hobby is collecting old engines and getting them to run. He asked me to salvage the engine as soon as possible. A few hours later a knock was heard at my door, and a shortwave listener of Cranberry Lake (also of Holland, New York), Mr. Leonard Crowley, came in and said, "Herb, let's go get the engine." At the same time my neighbor Harold DeVol, a skilled gunsmith, arrived and joined us. We went to Inlet, where I had a boat, and rowed to *The Beast's* grave. We tied a rope around the engine but could not budge it. It was bolted to the riverbed and would not let go. The next day Mr. Crowley brought a set of heavy duty come-alongs and several lengths of chain. We hooked the chain to a large balsam tree. After a mighty strain on our rigging, the engine pulled loose from its bed under the sand. Believe it or not, the piston, after having been under water since 1910, went up and down almost a full revolution when we turned the flywheel. We did not force it because the water pump was full of sand and we did not want to damage it. We took the engine to my garage in Wanakena and took the head off. It was shiny and clean inside. The muffler we unscrewed by hand, a 1¼-inch pipe fitting.

THE BEAST'S ENGINE TODAY

Overhauled after being under water for fifty years, the Truscott engine is now in smooth running condition.

(Courtesy Wesley Hammond)

Wes came and got the engine. We gave it to him, for we knew that he could put it in running order even though it had lain under water for over fifty years. It lacked a mixing valve. Hearing that the son of Mr. Burger, the builder of *The Beast,* lived in Black River and ran a machine shop, I went to see him. We had not met since we played together in our teens at Wanakena. He said that he had two mixing valves just like the one used on the old engine and would hunt them up in a few days. He was as good as his word, and I sent the two valves to Wes. They take the place of a carburetor, which could not be used on the make-and-break engine of the Truscott type.

78

Wes still had a long way to go to get the engine running. A section of the igniter was so badly corroded that it was impossible to see how it was made. An ad in a technical magazine asking for information on this part was answered by several persons who had similar engines. Wes went to see one of them and made a drawing and took pictures. Someone else loaned him a copy of *Harper's Magazine*, dated 1902, which had an ad illustrating the old Truscott engine. From this Wes was able to determine the location and the type of the oiler.

Wes then went to work building up the old igniter casting with weld, shaping it as in the illustrations he now had. He made new fingers, a push rod, points, and springs to complete the igniter. He ground the crankshaft and made new main bearings, a new piston pin, and its matching bushings. He honed the cylinder wall and filled all rusted out spots with epoxy putty. He made a new piston for the water pump and new valve seats for the brass balls used for valves. He replaced the cylinder head studs. The original muffler castings and the inside baffles of sheet metal were still good. Wes painted the engine and made an oak mounting for it to rest on. He then built a gas tank of copper.

Since the Truscott engine ran under a constant load and had no governor as such—only a spark advance governor—to allow for starting, it was necessary to put it under load. Wes welded up a water pump by using an old blower off a coal stoker and by attaching the pump to a barrel. By varying the opening in the exit of the blower pump, the load could be varied as desired. He then hooked up the pump to the old Truscott and belted the engine to an electric motor to "break in" a little. Now he was ready to start her up. It was a real thrill to get her to work, thanks to the efforts of many people.

This first engine to reach High Falls in 1908 or 1909 can now be seen running for three days every July at the Fairville engine show just outside of Newark, New York, on Route 88, where scores of engines and other interesting exhibits are on display.

The summer of 1910 saw another boat, the *Comet*, built for the yearly boat races on Cranberry Lake, that was really a success. It was the fastest boat on the lake for several years. It was powered with a forty horsepower, four-cylinder, two-cycle, three-port Roberts gasoline engine and made forty miles per hour. Its slender lines and the ease with which it rose up out of the water and flew along, leaving hardly any wake, put some modern craft, plodding through the water like rotary snowplows, to shame. Some of the modern boat designers could have got a few good ideas from her lines. A special boathouse for the

79

THE RYAN AND SCHLEDER LATH MILL
The mill was going strong in 1910.

(*Courtesy Mr. and Mrs. Keith Hamele*)

Comet was built on airtight empty wooden oil barrels with a canvas covered frame which allowed berthing at any desired place along the river frontage.

The year of 1910 Wanakena enjoyed one of its best seasons. It now had, besides the large sawmill which sawed 100,000 feet of lumber in a day, a lath mill, a whip butt mill, a barrel heading mill, a veneer mill, and a shoe last block factory that were all running full time. The Hotel Wanakena had over one hundred and fifty guests during the season.

An annual event that appealed to the hotel guests as well as the natives was the log rolling contest held every summer. Several men would get on a log in the water and with their calked shoes start it turning faster and faster until it was spinning rapidly. If the one man finally remaining on the log was able to bring it to a stop without falling off, he was declared the winner. A lively little old man from Wanakena by the name of Peter Akey won the contest for several years. No one ever could remain on the log with him, and when he finally got it spinning his legs traveled so fast it was a thrilling sight to see.

Another vacation came too soon to an end, and back home and to school I went. During the winter, as I ate homemade blueberry and raspberry pie from berries I had picked myself, and at other times, I wondered what would be the fate of the little village up in the Adirondacks that I loved so much. For the tree harvest on the Rich Lumber Company's 16,000 acres was coming to an end. Would the little settlement that had started as a lumber camp be able to survive as a village? Many people who had grown used to living in the forest wanted it to. But how would they make a living after the lumbering gave out?

11. LOGGING ENDS, RANGER SCHOOL BEGINS

It was June again, 1911, and I was looking out the window of the Carthage and Adirondack coach as it pulled into the Lake Bonaparte station, a little shanty by the wayside. Then through Jayville, where idle miners watched the train go by, and soon after, Benson Mines. I wondered what the crowd at the station would be doing tonight. The whistle sounded with a long blast as the engineer notified the conductor that the train was approaching a station. Huh, I thought, just as if the conductor didn't know when he got to the most important town on the whole C & A division. Benson Mines was a straight air stop, for the engine had to be spotted at the water plug. So the train usually stopped with a jolt. I didn't mind, for I was anxious to hear news of the town.

SPRUCE LATHS
Count them.   (*Courtesy Mr. and Mrs. Keith Hamele*)

AFTER THE EXPLOSION
  Note the missing smoke box door, which was blown out when the boiler of
the logging train engine exploded.

(Courtesy Mr. and Mrs. Keith Hamele)

  I soon learned there had been an explosion at Wanakena. A locomotive had blown up somewhere near the village. I couldn't wait to get to
Wanakena and find out the details. As soon as the train stopped at the
station there, I ran to my grandparents' home and asked them all about
it. Later I heard the story several times, and this is the way I remember
its being told. One of the old Shay geared locomotives, pulling a long
string of empty cars, was backing up the track toward the Plains. The
explosion took place about two miles from Wanakena on a fairly steep
part of the track. Low water in the boiler was the probable cause, but
no one could be sure.
  The fireman was killed, the engineer and a log train brakeman were
badly injured. A jewelry peddler was riding on a car next to the engine
with his sample case of wares. When the smoke box door blew off the
boiler, it struck him and severed his head from his body. A brakeman
riding on the last car was blown onto the track but only slightly injured.
An excitable person, he ran all the way to Wanakena for help.
  The explosion was heard plainly in the village. A couple of lady
guests from the hotel were walking up the railroad grade and met the

82

brakeman running toward the village. They asked him if anybody was killed. Without slowing his gait one bit, he answered, "Killed? I'm the only God damned survivor!" Many people spent hours looking for the jewel case, but no one ever admitted finding it.

During this summer all the shorter log railroad spurs were taken out. Only a few miles of track which went to the Plains and the Flow were left. In the autumn these tracks were also removed, for any logs which were left to be sawed were in the millpond at Wanakena. The jobbers left town. It looked as though Wanakena would suffer the same death as the lumbering towns the company had left in Pennsylvania and as many others in the Adirondacks. Thinking along this line and knowing that this was the last job the Rich Lumber Company was to undertake, the workers began to plan on something else to do after they had taken their last walk to town.

Wanakena had a little better chance to survive than those other lumbering towns, and for several reasons. During the early part of the town's existence, lots 75 feet wide and from 100 to 300 feet deep were laid out along both shores of the Oswegatchie River from the Rapids downstream for over a mile, at which point the company land joined the state-owned preserve. These lots were sold to anyone who had twenty-five dollars for a lot on the south side or fifty dollars for one on the north side of the river. The north-side lots were more desirable, for they were accessible by a narrow dirt wagon road which ran along their northern boundary line. The Hotel Wanakena was becoming famous. Many guests returned year after year for their annual vacations. A very popular man around town at this time was Billy Bean, the proprietor of the hotel. Billy, as he was known by all, had the knack of keeping his guests happy and entertained. The trout fishing continued to be very good, and many people had grown to love this cozy and beautiful little village. Their pride in it was shown by the neat lawns and flower beds around their homes. Thousands of blueberry and raspberry bushes were now growing in the lumbered area which had been slaughtered so terribly.

A very picturesque scene was to be found about a mile north of the hotel. It consisted of a high rock called Cathedral Rock above a beautiful, peaceful little body of water named Bean Pond by the hotel guests (now Eskar Pond). Many hotel guests took the short walk to see this scene as a practice trip for a hike to the Cat Mountain fire observation tower and return, a distance of over eleven miles. Trail lunches were prepared, and an entire day was taken up by these trips. Many people

83

who had never walked more than a few miles in any one day made these trips after a few weeks at the hotel. Several people over seventy years of age made the trip to Cat Mountain, to the amazement of the younger guests.

The summer of 1911 there was an elderly lady taking the trip on a hot day in July. She was very fond of watermelon and jokingly asked if it could be obtained when they reached Cat Mountain tower. Billy told her she needn't worry, for there would be watermelon when she finished climbing Cat Mountain. On these trips Billy always hired a guide to carry the basket of lunches and to prepare coffee in addition to making himself generally useful.

On this day Wilfred was hired to act as the guide. If he had started with his pack basket from the general store, he would have inspected its contents, for the clerks were always playing jokes on the guides if they left their baskets at the store for an order. Once Wilfred carried a railroad car coupling knuckle weighing over sixty pounds clear to High Falls. Most pack baskets had a rather small opening at the top in comparison to the diameter of the middle of the basket, but Wilfred had one with a large opening which would allow a five-gallon kerosene can to slide through. He left his basket at the hotel the night before the trip.

Watermelons were a rare thing in Wanakena in those days, but a shipment had just been received at the local meat market. Billy selected one which would just slip through the opening in Wilfred's basket. It was kept in the cooler all night and in the morning placed in a waterproof bag and packed with crushed ice. The top of the pack was covered over with a small tablecloth.

The party assembled shortly after seven in the morning on the hotel veranda, all eager to get started. Billy Bean introduced his guests to their guide. Wilfred was a shy man around strangers, but he was always anxious to be polite and gentlemanly. Over the years he had hit on a formula for acknowledging introductions that seemed to him just right. He used it over and over again, especially when ladies were present. He used it now: "I am very pleased to have you meet me."

Slinging the heavy pack to his back, Wilfred led off. He had filled up his corncob pipe with Warneke Brown tobacco, the strongest tobacco ever grown, and the smoke rose above his head and floated back over the heads of the party like a soft velvety cloud. After many resting periods, the long climb to the top of Cat Mountain was completed. The coffee-making equipment and the sandwiches were taken from a basket carried by one of the guests. Wilfred went to work preparing a fire while someone carefully spread out the tablecloth from Wilfred's basket. The stone fireplace where the coffee was brewing was in front of a little cabin in which the Cat Mountain fire observer lived with his wife and several small children.

During lunch Wilfred sat at one side talking with the observer, a French Canadian, in French. Meanwhile, the only guest of the party who knew about the watermelon took it out of Wilfred's basket and served it, ice cold, to the members of the party. It was a rare treat on the mountaintop but was served as though it was an everyday occurrence. One of the children who was watching the party eat said to his brother in French, "Look at the big pumpkin," for he had never seen a watermelon before. When Wilfred heard this and discovered what he had toted up the mountain on such a hot day, he said to the watchman, "Did you ever see a bigger damn fool dan I am?"

Wanakena now had a very good baseball field and a tennis court. Many interesting and exciting baseball games were played with the surrounding towns. One of the village's achievements, which people were proud of, was the suspension footbridge across the river at the foot of the Rapids. The distance between the supporting towers was 130 feet. The boards which one walked on had to be renewed quite often because of the lumbermen's calked shoes. The suspension bridge is still in use today, approached by a pretty, woodsy lane on each side.

Though Wanakena was only ten years old, people had already sunk roots here and considered it home. They remembered the good times they had had, the hunting and fishing, the berry picking, the trips up the river and out on the lake, and they looked forward to more of this. The hotel guests also had a stake in Wanakena and hoped that it would survive.

These thoughts were on my mind during the long winter and spring. It seemed as if the end of the school year in 1912 would never arrive. Just before it did, I broke my left arm at the elbow when a carpet pole I was using to pole-vault broke, and I landed on my extended arm with my feet pointing toward the sky. The first thing I asked when I came out of the chloroform was whether I would be able to go to the Adirondacks. In a few days the teacher wrote down the terribly dumb answers I gave her for the Regents questions, and then school was over for another year.

I arrived at Benson Mines with my arm in a sling. The train's arrival competed with a slow game of horseshoes for the evening's excitement. Soon the Cranberry Lake train to Wanakena took on its passengers,

85

mail, and express and I was on the last six miles of my journey again. The conductor told me a lot of news about the future of the village, and it all sounded bad.

When I reached my grandparents' house, the picture brightened. My grandfather told me of plans that were in the process of being realized. My uncle, J. Otto Hamele, the millwright, seemed to have more desire than anyone else to see Wanakena stay on the map. He had spent the entire winter making plans with the full cooperation of the Rich Lumber Company. When the company disbanded, two of its officials formed the Wanakena Company, which had just themselves as members.

Meanwhile, the Ford brothers, who owned the large sawmill, moved their machinery to Vermont. All the other mills closed down and their equipment was also moved out. When the evening whistle blew on the final day of operation, it seemed to die out with a penetrating, mournful wail and brought tears to the eyes of many people in the village. Just a few minutes before this, the pond men stood motionless and lost as they leaned on their pikepoles and watched the last log ride up the quivering old log chute to the top of the mill. The scaler's hands trembled as he gently scaled the final log and stroked his scale stick and decided then and there to take it home for his children to keep as a memento. The sawyer and his helpers watched the huge band saw turn to a slow easy stop never to turn again. The oiler had put on his last drop of lubrication. The fireman threw on his final shovel of fuel, and the dock men gently laid the last board upon the pile to dry. The workers marched out of the mill and across the swinging footbridge. The night watchman took over his duties only to see each night bringing his job nearer to an end. As the great sawmill was gradually torn down, the village was left without fire protection and without electric power. The fire hydrants were supplied by pumps at the mill which pumped the water from the river. The electric power, which was furnished by the special generator at the mill, slowed down to a final blackout.

Mr. Hamele had been with the lumber company during the whole time they were in operation on this project and had seen the great damage which had been done by lack of knowledge of proper lumbering methods. He had seen how the woods had been left after the lumber had been cut, with no effort to minimize fire hazard. He had seen the poor judgment used in the selection of trees to be cut and the complete lack of reforestation as the woods were slashed to pieces. He got the idea that there was a serious need for trained men who could supervise conservation of resources and lumbering operations. It seemed to him

86

THE ORIGINAL RANGER SCHOOL

The first students to arrive in September 1912 helped clear the site (1.7 miles from Wanakena) on Inlet Flow and construct the buildings. In 1928 a new and larger main building replaced the one above and was in turn enlarged by a new wing in 1961. The condition of clear ice with no snow is rare.

(Courtesy George Preston)

that right here in the wilderness was the place for just such an institution, which would teach common sense forestry and conservation.[14]

The lumber company officials readily agreed with Mr. Hamele that such a school was badly needed. They decided to donate 1,800 acres of their land to the New York State College of Forestry in Syracuse for immediate use. Buildings were erected and the first class got under way in the fall of 1912 at the New York State Ranger School, the first institution of its kind to be founded in North America. Today the school is operating with new modern buildings and equipment and is turning out large classes of men well trained for forest management and lumbering procedures. Students come from all over this country and abroad. In the present summer (1970), for instance, a group of Iowa students are enrolled for a special course of six weeks and for practical experience in a forest such as the tall corn state has never seen.

12. ABOUT HUNTING AND OTHER MATTERS

During my 1912 summer in the woods my parents moved to New York City, where I spent the following winter. After nine months in a city school I was more than ever anxious to get back to the mountains the following spring.

I found a greatly changed Wanakena the summer of 1913. The Cranberry Lake Railroad had given up its charter. The old locomotive was being used only to haul out machinery and the remaining cars of lumber. Passenger transportation to and from the village was now by a small gasoline-powered car and a rubberneck bus, which had been purchased in Buffalo. The original hard rubber tires were changed to flanged railroad wheels. These two rigs made the usual trips to meet the

REPLACEMENT FOR THE CRANBERRY LAKE RAILROAD
Along with an enclosed car, this rubberneck bus was converted for use on rails and ran between Wanakena and Benson Mines from 1913 till the tracks were removed in 1917.

(Courtesy Robert E. Keith)

train at Benson Mines. Village streets were now quiet and sleepy. The shouts of workmen and the clatter and whine of mill machinery were no longer heard. Many of the workers and several of the company officials had already left the area for other jobs, and more were to leave during this summer. Many houses were vacant. Some nice ten-room ones, completely furnished, were sold for two hundred and fifty to five hundred dollars. But a mile and a half out on the Flow the Ranger School was already growing, and many summer visitors continued to spend their vacations as usual at the hotel.

Wilfred spent considerable time at the hotel entertaining the front porch guests with his tales of adventure. One of his experiences the guests seemed to enjoy hearing about was how he outwitted a couple of game wardens who had been trying to catch him for having venison out of season. The wardens had been tipped off that Wilfred planned to go to a certain cove to pick up a basket of venison which had been left there for him to deliver to the Inlet House. So the wardens hid at the far end of the cove and waited for Wilfred to appear. Soon after dark they heard a canoe gently rub the sand shore and a slight splash of water. They moved out to catch up with Wilfred. They were confident they could outpaddle him and tried to do so. While he was rounding a sharp bend, he happened to look back and noticed a tiny light shining through the alders. He guessed he was being followed. The warden in the bow of the canoe had a small carbide lamp on his hat, for neither one of them knew the river well enough to paddle in complete darkness.

The race went on for several miles, Wilfred keeping just far enough ahead so the wardens could hear him across the loops in the river. When the race had only a mile to go, Wilfred speeded up. He gained enough time to stash his basket at a place on the bank, behind a big rock in a cave which had a very cold spring running in it and which kept fish and meat as well as an ice cooler. This place was known to only a few people and was called the Ice Box. Wilfred then paddled on beyond the regular landing, hid his canoe in the brush, and hurried back to the landing. There he grabbed an empty bait can and threw water on one of the canoes on the canoe rack. After dipping a paddle in the water to wet it, he hurried up to his room in the Inlet House. He took off his damp shoes and clothes and hid them and then put dry clothes beside his bed.

The wardens were sure of their prey as they landed and saw the fresh tracks on the shore and the wet canoe. They ran to the hotel and went straight to Wilfred's room, where they found him snoring. They in-

89

spected his clothes and were sadly convinced he was not the man they had been chasing. Waking up the proprietor, they got his permission to search the other rooms. Nothing was found. The wardens got a room of their own and stayed the rest of the night. When they departed in the morning, Wilfred gave them a pleasant "Come again."

Another guide and good friend of Wilfred's, Walter Gates, was a very large man and extremely powerful. A jobber who had moved out what he wanted from his last camp at the east end of the Plains gave Wilfred a couple of bed springs and mattresses and also told him he could have anything else he might find around the camp. At this time Walter was helping Wilfred with his camp work. The two of them paddled up to Carter's Landing carrying an old wheelbarrow in the canoe. They wheeled the barrow across the Plains to the lumber camp and put the springs and mattresses on it. Wilfred spied an old grindstone and said, "We will take dat," so it was added to the load. As they walked by the old blacksmith's shop, Gates said, "We had better take the old forge along, for it is in good shape," so they loaded it on and started out. Wilfred kept looking at the old forge riding on top of the load. Finally he made Walter stop with "My lan, we forgot de anvil," so they went back and threw on the anvil. One man wheeled the barrow while the other balanced the load, and then they changed.

About a half mile from their boat was a muddy stretch in the trail. Their barrow sank in it just about up to the frame. Gates said, "Now we will make a hand barrow out of it and I will see what kind of man you are." They walked back to the old lumber camp and found some suitable poles and plenty of hay wire. After much wiring, the poles were secured to the wheelbarrow. The men were ready to proceed. "I will give you the light end so you can't squawk," Gates said as he tested the weight. There was no noticeable difference. They struggled on through the mud. Later in the summer when the mire had dried like a plaster of paris cast, their tracks remained in the trail over a foot deep. After they got on to dry ground, neither would suggest that they put the barrow down and wheel the load, so they kept on carrying it. They met some guests from another camp who asked them, "Why don't you wheel the load?" Wilfred replied, "De big gent is trying to make de fool out of me, but when we get dere he will be de big one."

Later during the summer I was sitting on Wilfred's porch one warm evening along with several other guides and the conversation drifted around to the approaching hunting season. It was well known that Walter Gates had a habit of making drives for his parties without making any noise. He would sometimes walk stealthily out on a runway where a watcher had been stationed. Wilfred said, "Walter, some day one of your party will shoot you for a deer. So far you've had men who shoot only when dey see a buck wid horns." A couple of years later Gates gave up the High Falls camp he was running and went to operate a hunting lodge near Cranberry Lake village. One day he walked out on a runway and was shot through the heart by a stupid hunter.

Wilfred didn't like to see any wild thing killed needlessly, and I doubt if he ever killed over five or six deer in his whole life. He was quite different from some of the riffraff that come here today and kill everything that runs, walks, crawls, creeps, swims, or flies, even killing some of the children's pets that stray a few feet beyond the village limit. He guided a few hunting parties, but most of his time was spent doing work around camps and paddling the deer which the hunters killed down to the Inlet House landing. He always saved the deer skins and heads whenever he could get them, however. He would tack them up on a large tree and think about them later on, only to find they were spoiled. One time a sport told Wilfred that he would like a nice set of buck horns to hang over the fireplace mantel in his den at home. Wilfred replied, "Come wid me and we will go and get dem. I have just what you want." When they arrived at the tree where Wilfred had hung them up, there was only a little hair to be found. The sport asked, "When did you hang the head up?" "I guess it was tree yar ago dis fall," Wilfred replied. Time meant nothing to him until he reached old age and began brooding about its passing.

One time a venison supper was planned a few weeks before the season opened. Wilfred was asked to paddle a certain person down the river after dark to jack a deer. In the early days jacking was quite common. Deer like to wade around and feed in the river at night. It was easy to paddle quietly up to them. A hunter armed with an old shotgun and with a carbide lamp fixed to his hat sat in the bow of the canoe. The deer would pay no attention to the light. If they did not get a scent or hear a noise, they were easy prey for the hunter. A few miles down the river on this particular night Wilfred and his party spied a nice buck eating the tender grass which grew underwater. The deer was killed with dispatch and dragged up on the river bank. As usual Wilfred asked if he could have the hide and head. He was given them, and while the innards and other parts were being buried, he hung up the hide on the alders back away from the bank where it couldn't be seen. Since he did this with only a dim carbide lamp for light, he didn't spend

91

much time looking around. Several days later as he was paddling up the river with another guide and as the canoe rounded a sharp bend onto a long straight stretch, his friend said, "Look, Wilfred, there is a buck ahead of us." The buck had a queer look, however, and as they got nearer to it they could see it had no legs. Slowly it dawned on Wilfred that he had walked right straight across a sharp bend and hung his deer hide on the river bank in plain sight. "We'd better bury dat stuff," he said, "or de warden will see it and blame me. I wonder who de fool was dat done dat."

I guess that to completely round out a summer in the Adirondacks one should taste a piece of jerked venison. Most guides indulged a little in such forbidden game taken in the summer. There were many ways of providing the guests with such a delicacy. One example is as follows: First, you must kill a suitable deer which should not be a fawn, an old dry doe, a doe with fawn, or an old tough buck. A yearling deer is about right, and it should not be killed until after July Fourth, for up until this time deer are still lean from the long hard winter. After this date they have their red coats and the buck's horns are in velvet.

When you have selected and killed your deer, hang it up in a tree and skin off the hide. Then lay the hide on the ground with the hair side down. Cut all the meat into chunks and strips, lay it on the hide, and liberally salt and pepper it. Then wrap it up carefully, being sure to keep the hair side out, and bury it under moss, in a cool spot, until the following night. Go to camp and get a good night's rest.

In the morning prepare your jerking rack. From here on almost everyone uses a different system. If you use the following one, I am sure you won't be disappointed. A roll of fine mesh chicken wire about six feet long and the width of the length of a common stove pipe will hold all the meat from a medium sized deer. From your tinsmith purchase a piece of the stove-pipe material rolled up in one piece as long as your six feet of chicken wire. (This stove-pipe material is a refinement and can be omitted.) Drive some stakes in the ground, line them with stones, and nail some poles across them; then stretch the piece of chicken wire about sixteen inches from the ground, from which you have scraped off the loose topsoil. Now your sheet metal should be secured about six or seven inches above the wire to reflect the heat and keep off the rain and the dirt if the weather turns bad. Plenty of dry wood is required and preferably lots of dry hemlock bark if available. Green birch or black cherry wood will make good coals and also furnish plenty of smoke and heat to flavor the meat, as is preferred by some people. It will require

92

from three to eight hours of smoking, according to your skill and patience.

You are of course in violation of the game laws in regard to the time of year you killed this deer, so you may have trouble with the game wardens. Select a secluded place and don't light your fire until after dark, for the fire warden may see the smoke and send men to put out the forest fire. When the fire is lighted, it is regulated by sprinkling a little water on it with a piece of evergreen bough to avoid its flaring up and scorching the meat. The process needs a nice bed of coals and lots of heat with moderate smoke.

Now you know how, but please don't do it out of season, for no other reason than that your meat may cost you as much per pound as prime porterhouse. You can have nearly as much fun by using some veal and throwing on some brook trout for a treat. If you should want a little variety, bring a hand-operated meat grinder out to your jerking rack. To help pass away the time as your meat is being prepared, grind up some salt pork and raw venison, take some prepared sausage seasoning, mix to suit your taste, seal in mason jars, and bury in the cool moss. In a few days try some with your morning pancakes. It does wonders for your constitution. After a couple of weeks on this kind of food, when you get out of the woods you will ride on merry-go-rounds with the kids.

WILFRED MORRISON SMOKING HIS WARNEKE BROWN
Wilfred and an unidentified assistant saw logs to rebuild Bert Dobson's camp at Wanakena.   (*Courtesy Pearl Morrison*)

Each summer for several years the guides in the Cranberry Lake region held contests, generally at Nunn's Inn on Cranberry Lake. They demonstrated the skills required of a guide, like paddling a canoe, fly casting, and rescuing persons in the water. One event which the guides were most anxious to win was a paddling race with something added. They were to paddle from Nunn's dock to a certain island on which each guide had already prepared a coffee can half full of water, hanging from a suitable arrangement of crotched sticks and a pole. Kindling wood had been laid under the can. Each guide had his own method of arranging his fuel so it would burn best for him. The winner of the race was the first guide to paddle to the island, light his fire, and get his can of water to boil. The judges of the contest inspected the cans to be sure they were all filled to the correct level. Wilfred won this contest every year by a narrow margin. One day long after these contests were discontinued, he told me how he had managed to put one over on the rest of the guides. "Just before de water was ready to bile," he told me, "I drop a small piece of carbide in de can which make it bile. Den I yell for de judge to take a look and make me de winner."

Wilfred was known as the most polite person in this section of the Adirondacks. He never swore while guiding a party, and his general manners were admired by everyone who knew him. One day Bert Dobson was paddling one of his fly fishermen guests when he came to a sharp bend above the Morrison Spring Hole. He could hardly believe his ears, for the air was blue with profanity and terrible name calling directed at a person who was continually getting his flies hung up in the alders along the bank. Bert soon recognized Wilfred's voice and was reluctant to move around the bend. When he did slide the canoe gently around, there was Wilfred standing up in the stern of his Peterborough with his head completely hidden in the thick alders trying to unhook his guest's flies and swearing like a madman. Bert was flabbergasted but finally said, "Why, Wilfred, what on earth is the matter with you, treating your guest in such a disgraceful manner? It's not like you at all." Wilfred replied, "By de Jeezus, I have alway want to tell dis gent off who fish for bird stead of trout. Dis is de happiest day of my life." After a pause he continued, "Dis gent is stone deaf."

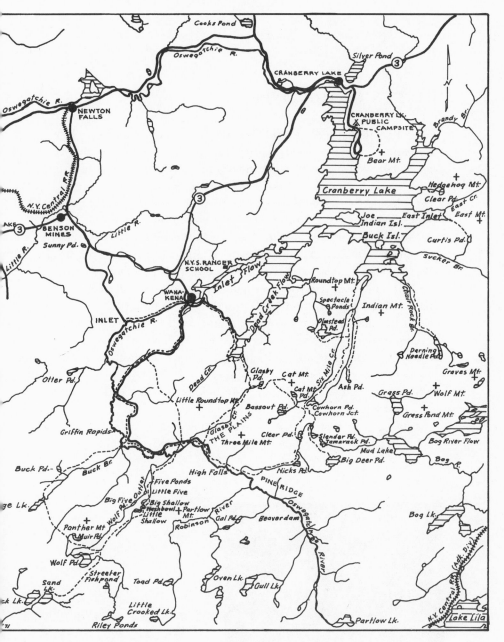

The Oswegatchie (East Branch) and Cranberry Lake Region. (Adapted by
George Bowditch from a 1970 trail map compiled by the New York State
Department of Environmental Conservation, Bureau of Forest Recreation)

95

13. FUN UP THE RIVER

After finishing school in 1914, I worked for several months in New York, but summers in the woods had spoiled me for city life. During the winter of 1915 I decided to make the big break. In late spring of that year I moved to Wanakena to make it my permanent home, knowing that making a living there would sometimes be touch and go. Guiding was a seasonal occupation, and the mills had closed down. But I knew, just the same, that the village in the woods was the right place for me. Except for brief intervals of work elsewhere and several years of service in World Wars I and II, I have spent the rest of my life in Wanakena.

The same year I settled permanently there, the Inlet House changed hands. Loren Moore and his wife, Mary, purchased the place and became the new hosts on the Inlet. Mary was a fine cook and Pop, as her husband soon came to be called, was an excellent fly fisherman and fisherman's guide. He was a large man whose strength and endurance seemed to have no limit. When you shook hands with him, you felt that a bear had hold of you. He came to be known as the Paul Bunyan of the Oswegatchie.

During my first winter in Wanakena and the Moores' first at the Inlet House, I got to know them well. One day when the snow was over

LOREN AND MARY MOORE
The proprietors of Inlet House in Sunday dress are standing in front of a pile of hemlock bark, which Loren used to buy and sell, in his backyard at Inlet.

knee high, the phone rang at the general store and Pop Moore was on the line. He wanted someone to come to Inlet and help him cut and store ice. His hired man had left him, the road to Benson Mines was too deep for old Pat, his faithful horse, and the town would not get around to plowing him out for several days. He had uncovered the ice on the river and found it to be two feet thick. My uncle suggested that I take his snowshoes and go to Inlet to help Mr. Moore.

I hiked up the two-mile trail. As soon as I arrived, we began working on the ice, sawing it into cakes about two feet square. It was too thick to spud, so we had to saw each side. We pulled the cakes out and loaded them onto a sleigh, which old Pat drew up to the icehouse. We were a week filling the icehouse because Mr. Moore supplied not only himself but also the two cottages across the river with ice for the summer. I was glad when the sawing was over. It was the hardest kind of work I had ever done. Mary apologized for the first dinner, saying that she had not been prepared for company. "All I have this noon," she said, "is fried salt pork, baked potatoes, milk gravy, and blueberry pie." "Please don't change the menu," I replied. "I'll never get sick of such a meal."

For breakfast we had delicious pancakes, sausage, and maple syrup. I noticed a large pile of pancakes on the stove after we had finished eating and asked Mary why she had made so many. "These are for our guest," she replied. "Loren, go get him." Loren opened a door and in came a Great Dane. Mary threw a cake at a time to the big dog. Each disappeared at one fast gulp. She said the dog belonged to Dr. Calkins, who owned the camps across the river, and that she was boarding it for the winter.

I stayed a second week and helped Loren cut wood. By the time I left, the town had plowed out his road and brought in his mail. After bidding them goodbye, I took off for Wanakena on snowshoes. Some time later my uncle met Mr. Moore at Benson Mines and asked how his nephew had made out. Mr. Moore said, stretching the truth, "He was the best worker I ever had."

Mary Moore was quite a penny pincher, as one of the guests at Inlet House soon found out. Father Lynch, from a city downstate, spent several summer vacations there. When it came time to settle his bill, he would say to Mary, "How much is the damage?" She always had a long bill made out and charged for every small item she could think of. Father Lynch would say nothing as he wrote out a check. One Sunday Mary had a bad attack of rheumatiz in her knees and asked the priest if he would say Mass for her, for she was in such pain that she could not stand the trip to the Benson Mines church. Father Lynch complied readily. The next Sunday she asked the same favor and also the Sunday following, which was the last of Father Lynch's vacation. When Mary handed him the large bill, he took a little more time than usual looking it over. Then he wrote something on the bill and made out his check. When he handed the bill and check to Mary, a startled look came over her face. She read, "Saying Mass, three Sundays at $20 each, $60." From that time on, Mary had no more crippling rheumatiz on Sundays. Father Lynch's bills were just as big as ever, but he kept coming back, perhaps for Mary's pancakes.

One day my friend Johnny Tender, the Wanakena plumber, and I were having a cup of coffee in Mary's kitchen. The hot water tank was leaking. It was clear that some of the old piping needed to be replaced. Mary was moaning about the expense of sending to Carthage for a plumber. Johnny said, "Herb and I will fix it for you and save you money." "I guess you won't," Mary snapped. "I don't want any half-assed plumbing in my kitchen."

About a month later we were again sitting in her kitchen having doughnuts and coffee before going up the river. All of a sudden her hot water tank began to pound and shake. Mary was quite upset over the

JOHN TENDER AND TROUT
Johnny, Wanakena's plumber, is holding an eight-pound brown trout caught by the author on June 6, 1920, in the Rapids. Johnny's clothes were usually paint spotted.

noise. Johnny looked over the hook-up and found what the trouble was. He said nothing about it to Mary but told her we would fix it for $20; she would not have to pay if the noise continued. She reluctantly told us to go ahead. The next time we visited Inlet we brought the plumbing tools along and made the necessary repairs in an hour's time. There was no noise now. Mary grudgingly gave us the $20. "What a fool I was," she said, "paying the plumber from Carthage his transportation and board and big wages for a poor job." Then she added, perking up, "I'll have to charge you double for the coffee and doughnuts."

On one occasion, though, Mary took my side in a dispute over wages between Loren and me. Loren had purchased ten cords of kitchen stove wood from a farmer in Fine and had asked me how much I would charge to deliver it in the truck I was operating at that time. I gave him a fair price and he agreed to it. When my helper and I drove up to his back door, he showed us where he wanted the wood unloaded. I had a stake and rack body with a hoist. I raised up the ten cords after taking out the tail gate, and the wood slid across his back door. "I won't pay the price you asked!" he roared. "I didn't know you had a dumper." But Mary came to our rescue. "You old fool," she shouted. "What difference does it make how they unloaded it? They worked hard enough loading it."

The Moores had many noted and interesting guests at Inlet. From a small city a few miles north of New York an unusual guest arrived one day in early spring. He hired a canoe and rented a room, saying, "I'll paddle up the river, and if I like it I will stay until September." He evidently liked the river and the woods, for he came back every summer for over ten years. Mr. Homburg was a great scholar and a disciple of Izaak Walton. While in England he had purchased a lot of fine trout fly fishing equipment. Each year he came he also brought fifteen gallons of whiskey with him. During most of his time in the woods he camped out, setting up his tent just below the Root Hole near Wolf Creek Spring Hole. A large leaning balsam tree on the river's edge furnished a back rest for the rustic chair in which he spent considerable time reading and studying. He found some dry poles, made a frame around his favorite sitting place, and covered it with fine mosquito netting. Each morning one could find him sitting inside the netting, reading and enjoying his morning cups of coffee, into which he poured some of his choice whiskey. If you happened along, you would be invited to have a "coffee royal" with him.

Wilfred very often happened to pass by at the right time. When he

99

returned to camp, he would always say, "Dat Humbug gent is a very nice man." Wilfred knew of the cache of whiskey and one day said, "I wonder where dat gent keep his moose milk."

Just a few rods above Homburg's tent was Pop Moore's summer fishing camp, which was composed of several tents with wooden floors. On the bank of the river above the high water mark was an old beer keg in an upright position, buried in the ground for about one third its length. This keg had been there many years and the bung was securely driven in. Being in the shade, the keg had not dried out enough to leak. It was a favorite seat for fishermen, and its top was well polished from constant use.

The first year Homburg camped out he began looking for a suitable place where he might hide his whiskey and be able to make many trips to it without making a new trail. When he first saw the keg, he realized it was not likely to be disturbed as it was very useful as a seat. After carefully prying out the bung, he inspected the keg and found it leak proof, dry, and clean inside. He drove the bung back in and made sure it would not come out easily. Then he moved one of the iron bands and drilled a hole large enough to insert a small rubber hose. He placed a funnel on one end of the hose and poured his fifteen gallons of whiskey into the large beer keg. When he wanted to fill his service bottle, he used this same hose as a siphon and would slide the band back over the hole when he was through filling his bottle.

One time after Mr. Homburg's untimely death Wilfred and Pop Moore were talking at Pop's camp. In fact, Wilfred was sitting on the beer keg smoking his Warneke Brown. "Did you ever find out," Pop asked, "where Homburg kept his moose milk?" Wilfred said, "No, dat was a clever sport, he fool me." Pop went on, "Wilfred, you are sitting on the hiding place." Wilfred peeked at him from under his battered felt hat and with a woebegone look said, "Do you mean dat?" Pop told him to push the top band up a bit and smell. Wilfred hurried to do so. When he took a sniff, he almost cried. "Curse of Chri," he said, "what is de matter wid me I could not smell dat before?" Old Pop was the only one who had known where the moose milk was hidden.

The guides I knew were honest men. You could leave things on the river bank in plain sight and go back and find them a week later. Everything except whiskey, that is. There was a sort of silent agreement that whiskey left in the woods was common property, a fair prize for anyone lucky or clever enough to find it. There was one guide, though, even in the good days, who got a bit out of hand. Just before the height of the trout season he used to place a set of bedsprings in the deep pool under High Falls. When no one was around, he pulled them out and picked off a nice collection of fishing tackle. We admired his cleverness, but it made us uneasy. I guess it was the first symptom of decline.

One winter in February a summer visitor came up to see what conditions were like in midwinter. He asked Wilfred to take him to some pond where he could fish through the ice and also have a try at walking on snowshoes. Wilfred asked several of us to join in the hike. We found out later that he had asked us so we could help break trail rather than for our sociability. We all had a good time, though.

We went to Toad Pond, east of Dead Creek Flow. When we got there, we found a huge beaver house at the edge of the pond. While still several rods away, Wilfred said, "Ha! dey are home, see de smoke from de chimney." Later as we were eating our lunch by the warm fire, he told us that beavers leave a vent through the sticks and mud at the top of their houses. On a cold day the warm moisture seeping through causes a slight wisp of steam to rise from the house. He said he learned that from the Indians in northern Canada.

The wind had blown the snow from the ice by the house. Wilfred felled a couple of dead tamarack trees on this clear spot. He then cut up the limbs so he had a fine pile of wood for a fire. The rest of us cut the trunks into lengths for seats so we could eat our lunch in comfort in front of the fire. Wilfred called the sport over to the pile of branches and said, "Now I will show you how Daniel Boone start de fire out in de cold snow on a wet day." The sport watched carefully as if expecting to learn some great secret, only to see Wilfred reach in his hip pocket and pull out a pint whiskey bottle filled with kerosene, which he poured all over the sticks before touching a match to it. Then he said, "Dere is de real McCoy."

One time Wilfred was paddling in the river with a large fat man, who weighed over two hundred and twenty pounds, in the bow of the canoe. An old rusty shotgun whose stock had been patched with friction tape lay across the man's knees, and a faint glimmer from a carbide light pierced the darkness. Wilfred skillfully shook the boat as a signal for the man to be alert, for there was game around the next bend. The hunter carefully and quietly raised the weapon from his knees as two little eyeballs reflected like diamonds from the tiny flame of the lamp. The canoe glided ahead until it looked as though it would hit the shining eyes. Then a dull swishy sound like a skyrocket broke the still night. The old gun's report sounded weak, but the young buck fell into the mud at the river's edge. The fat man stepped out of the canoe, picked up the deer in his arms like a sack of potatoes, and carried it up the bank. He had just reached the top of the bank when the buck came to. Its four feet flew in all directions. The man didn't dare let go. Wilfred yelled, "Hang on to him, Walter, hang on to him, he's no bigger dan you." The big man yelled back, "Shoot him, shoot him." It was over in a minute, for the buck got loose enough to give a big kick that sent the hunter flying into the brush. The old shells had no power left and had only stunned the deer. "The shells are too old," Wilfred said. "I fix dat." He took the wadding out of two shells, poured all the powder into one shell, replaced the wad, and said, "De next buck will stay down." Once again the canoe glided down the river. Several miles downstream, another pair of eyes. A terrific blast, and a large hunter lying flat on his back in the bottom of the canoe. Wilfred said, "Dere, by de Jeezus. You will have no trouble wid dat one."

The 16,000 acres of lumbered-off forest were becoming a great tax burden on the Wanakena Company's maintenance account. There was no revenue from this land. But several pulpwood jobbers were trying to buy it. The spruce and balsam that had been too small for cutting had grown to a size which was of interest to the pulpwood men. They would have cut everything, even down to pikepole size, if the company had sold the land to them. Many people wanted to buy land at High Falls and the Plains, but the company would not break the land into pieces. The sportsmen and summer guests of the area were very much concerned as to the disposition of the land. Someone suggested that perhaps the State of New York would be interested in buying it to add to the Adirondack preserve. After much dickering the land was finally purchased by the state in 1919. Its future now seemed secure from lumbering and other earth-stripping projects. Almost everyone agreed that this was the proper way to keep the woods as wild as possible.

Wilfred felt bad, however, for no permanent buildings were allowed on state land. Eventually, his camp was burned down along with the other guides' camps, and with it went his spirit and desire to guide in the woods. The best of the naturally wild days of the Adirondacks were coming to an end. The camp at High Falls was torn down, and a regulation state open camp, or lean-to, was erected on the site. Other lean-tos were built and were now open to the public, free. The longest period of time any one party could occupy one of these camps was three days in succession. Sometime before its acquisition of former Rich Lumber Company land, the state had already acquired adjoining tracts on the east, west, and south. Today it owns a broad band of forest preserve in southern St. Lawrence County, including, in the Town of Fine, about half of Township 14 and all of Township 15 except the 2,330 acres of Ranger School land, the village of Wanakena, and a few tiny inholdings; and in the towns of Clifton and Colton to the east, most of the shoreline of Cranberry Lake and many of the outlying ponds south of the lake. These ponds, such as Cowhorn, Cat Mountain, Bassout, Clear, and Glasby, were formerly in a large tract leased by the Indian Mountain Club, with headquarters at Nunn's Inn, and were all posted. Fishing was restricted even among club members, and outsiders were kept off the land by guides hired to patrol the lines. Each year one pond of the group was opened for fishing by the members. The ponds were thus given a chance to reproduce fish naturally, and fishing remained excellent.

South of the St. Lawrence County line, adjoining the above-mentioned tracts, was the 75,000-acre Webb Purchase of 1896, in which the state acquired land in northeastern Herkimer and northwestern Hamilton counties. Fifty thousand acres of this were primitive forest which had never been lumbered. The ponds of this remote area seemed to keep themselves stocked because they weren't overfished. In Five Ponds, Muir Pond, Wolf Lake, Toad Pond, Streeter Fishpond, Riley Ponds, and Sand Lake, trout up to three pounds could be caught in summer. Big Deer Pond, also south of the county line, was not much of a trout pond but became famous because deer congregated there during the summer months. Its shore is of hard bluish colored sand. One can walk several rods into the pond before reaching a depth of four feet. It seemed that on hot days during July and August one could see as many as fifty deer at a time playing and cooling off in this pond, especially when the deerflies were bad and there was no wind. When the deerflies were really biting, the deer would run from the woods right into the water, making it fly. This was a pretty sight. The pond was a deer paradise. Big deer, little deer, bucks, does, and spotted fawns all played together. When the summer was over, they all scattered to avoid the hunters.

These deer had a good break, for near Big Deer Pond was an abandoned lumber camp occupied by a quaint old character named Fide Scott. He loved the deer and kept summer poachers away. He kept a cow, a dog, and a cat, and when he came to Wanakena for supplies he used the cow as a pack horse. He put a bag on the cow's back and divided the load evenly on each side. As he left town with his cow and pets, the summer guests enjoyed watching him and his family. He always had something in the supplies for each of his pets. Occasionally some of the more hardy guests at the hotel would make the trip to Big Deer Pond and stay overnight at Fide's camp. Fide was always glad to have them as his guests, for the slight fee he charged for their meals was always augmented by generous tips.

One spry old lady who was a guest at the hotel made these trips whenever she could find someone to go with her. One time she and the others were seated at the table eating breakfast, which consisted of pancakes, sausage, and maple syrup. "Uncle Fide," she asked, "why have you put caraway seed in the cakes this morning?" Without looking up from his stove, Uncle Fide replied, "Damn, those mice have been in the flour again."

Some days one could see black smoke drifting from the old, tottering, rusty tin smoke pipe which stuck out of the roof of the former blacksmith shop at the camp where Fide lived. When you approached the

PHILO SCOTT AND COMPANIONS
Uncle Fide with his cow, Betsy, who doubled as a pack horse, and his dog, Christmas. The house is believed to be Fide's winter home (no longer standing) at Scott's Bridge. Once, on the trail to Big Deer Pond, Betsy, who never got used to the deep woods, had an attack of bush fever and went on a rampage. This photo was sold as a postcard at the Rich and Andrews Store, where stories about Uncle Fide circulated freely.

104

camp, you could hear the ring of the hammer on the anvil, but when you tried the door it would be locked from the inside. Uncle Fide would come out and talk to you after locking the door. Once when he was away someone ransacked the place. After that he took no more chances of leaving his treasure alone, and when he made his trips to Wanakena for supplies he always took the object he was working on with him, all wrapped up in burlap and tucked away in his packsack. He finally finished the item and brought it into town to display his handiwork to the townsfolk. It was what he called a "mad ax" and is known as a mattock. Whether he was successful in getting a patent was always a matter of debate.

Uncle Fide took some of the best logs from the old lumber camp, which had begun to fall down, and built one of the most cozy and beautiful small log cabins one could ever see in the Adirondacks. The floor was made of hand hewn, diamond shaped blocks, about one foot thick and laid together to form a very interesting pattern. This floor was as smooth and even as one could want. Many articles of his furniture were beautiful examples of craftsmanship.

When Uncle Fide passed away, this land was acquired by the state, and the Indian Mountain Club had to give up its lease. During the winter when the snow was right for sleighing, Fide's little cabin was torn down and carefully hauled by sleigh to Nunn's Inn at the head of Cranberry Lake. At this location it was reassembled exactly as old Fide had built it, a monument to men of his character who are fast disappearing from the woods.[15]

14. JIM WELCH

Just a few rods from Deremos Point near the head of Cranberry Lake nestled a cozy cottage amid the tall green timber. Almost any time of the year one could see smoke curling out of the tall brick chimney. Jim Welch made this Adirondack camp his forest home and commuted several times a year from Sandy Creek, New York, where he and his family lived for many years. Jim was about five feet ten inches in height and weighed about one hundred and sixty pounds. His hair was snow white, his eyes dark, and his face beamed with a ruddy complexion.

When I first met him, Jim was in his late fifties. Every task he undertook he carried on with a calm, fixed determination to make it worthy of a master craftsman, which he was whether at work or play. One time when I was helping him repair a camp on Cranberry Lake, he handed me a board to saw where he had marked it. I was careless and didn't follow the line. When he saw what I had done, he said, "Herby, always try to do every job a little bit better than the other fellow, and soon your day's work will be something to look forward to with pleasure." I never knew a person who loved his work as he did.

Shortly after I met him he stopped in at my cottage on the river for a bit of lunch before he continued his row down the river to his own cottage. He had a small boy with him and said proudly, "Here is my son, Fay. I have brought him up here with me to see if the Adirondack air will sharpen his appetite, for he doesn't eat as he should and I am worried about him." The next day he rowed all the way to my place to borrow some medicine for the boy. In a short while the wonderful mountain air took the place of the lad's medicine, and he grew as he should.

Jim was the best otter trapper and hunter that ever came to this section. He would find a fresh hole in the ice where an otter had come out to breathe, and then he would build a blind on runners, which consisted of material natural to that particular location. He would draw his blind near the hole and wait for an otter to appear.

One fall during the first part of the hunting season I was invited to spend a few days at his cottage and to hunt deer with him. When I arrived at his place, he said, "There is an old man staying here with me who is quite an odd person. He has brought his own food and cooks separately, even to his tea. You be sure to use my butter, salt, pepper, etc., and not eat any of his food." The two men always ate together but seldom spoke.

Right after the supper dishes were finished, Jim told me we had better go to bed, for we would get up early in the morning to hunt. I found an old magazine and read by the light of a kerosene lamp until I became tired enough to fall asleep. It seemed like just a few minutes when I heard a voice booming up the stairway. "Daylight in the swamp, the nights are of vast length, the days are a mere nothing" was the call I heard. I jumped out of bed, groped for the matches, and burned my hand on the lamp chimney. When the light was lit, I found my pants were still swinging on the chair back.

After a heavy breakfast we went back of the camp a few rods, where an arm of the lake extended into the woods and formed a protected har-

106

JIM WELCH—HUNTER, TRAPPER, GUIDE

On the back porch of Forest Home, Jim is shown with two of his favorite guns, an old Ithaca 10-gauge shotgun (front) converted to rifle and shot—"a great game getter" in his words—and a more modern 12-gauge Remington automatic (leaning against door). Two "partridges" (ruffed grouse) hang at the right of the door.

(Courtesy Fay Welch)

bor. We got into Jim's tiny skiff. As he started to row, he said, "We will go around the point as I want to look at some traps. Then we can cut across to the hunting trail, where I will show you how the old man gets his deer each season." After a short row we landed and then walked a piece until we came to a beaten trail about one mile back into the woods on a large peninsula. Jim said, "Soon as we get around the bend in the trail ahead, look sharp and see if you can spot the old man, for he will be there looking at you."

When we arrived at the bend, I looked but could see no one. Old Jim laughed and said, "Stop here. You are now within one rod of the old man." I still could not imagine where he could be unless he was in a treetop. I asked if he was. "No," Jim said, "his feet are on the ground, but you aren't the first one to have trouble finding him." He motioned

107

toward some evergreen trees and told me the old boy was sitting behind them. We went nearer, and Jim showed me the entrance to the old man's hiding place. A bunch of dry poles had been fastened together making a wigwam, which each year he cleverly covered over with green spruce and balsam boughs. He had built a comfortable seat with a cushion and a table on which to eat and play solitaire as he waited for his buck. He had made portholes on all sides through which he could see to shoot. The idea for this blind had occurred to him after he had got too old to roam around the woods. Each year he had used the blind he had taken home a nice buck. I found that if Jim killed a deer before the old man did or if a deer he killed was larger, the old man wouldn't speak to Jim for days afterward.

After we left I asked Jim if it made the old man mad for us to walk around his blind, but Jim said that he liked to have hunters around to chase the deer past his hiding place. We saw no buck that day. When we arrived back at the skiff, Jim laughed, for we found tracks all around the boat where a big buck had nosed around.

While at the cottage I had the pleasure of seeing the mementos of some very big trout that had been caught off the large dock in front of the cottage. Records of many great trout catches were made on brown paper by tracing the outline of the fish on it. Then it was cut out and the fisherman's name, the weight of the trout, and the date were written on the paper, which was pasted between the studs. In some cases these cutouts just fitted between the two-foot center studding. A few had to be hung in other places in the room so they would not curl up.

One morning when Jim was rowing along the lake shore looking at his traps, he spied a large black bear lumbering out of the water up onto Haywood Hawk's Island. The bear had come from Joe Indian Island. Jim landed and followed the bear across the little island. The bear jumped into the lake again and started to swim toward Kimball Island. Jim shot him in the water. He dressed out the bear and then rolled him into the skiff and rowed back to camp. With the aid of an old wheelbarrow and by tugging and lugging, he finally got the bear hung up on the front porch.

At supper the old man asked Jim if he had had any luck, and when Jim said he had the old man pretended he wasn't interested. That evening, however, the old gent wouldn't talk, so Jim knew he had seen the bear.

In his younger days Jim was a noted musician and played for dances. He was a very fine trap shooter and had competed with many

108

good shots. I stopped at his home in Sandy Creek once when he was in his seventies and found him soaking his hands in kerosene oil. He said that he was limbering up his fingers so he could play in an old fiddlers' contest in Syracuse. A neighbor had entered but was too sick to attend. Jim was going in his place and was using his name as a contestant. Jim won. His neighbor won by proxy and was as happy as though he had played himself.

15. THE LEARYS

Art Leary and his family were newcomers but made a name for themselves in Wanakena. They moved to the village in 1914. After looking over the vacant houses, they chose a desirable building and started a small hotel, catering mostly to fishermen and hunters and operating at seasons when the Hotel Wanakena was closed.

Art was of slight build, five feet eight in height. He had blue eyes and was quite bald. He had lost his right thumb, and his left hand was also crippled. But one had to look sharply to notice that he didn't have full use of his hands.

The Leary Hotel was run by Art's sister Bessie, by another sister, Belle, and, as long as they lived, by their parents, while Art himself took care of the fishermen and hunters that wanted to visit remote parts of the woods. Art and his father, Bill, were not always on good terms. Once they quarreled over a sleigh I had sold to Bill. It was worth a quarrel. I had ordered it from a fine wagon and sleigh maker in Star Lake named Isaiah Walker. He was getting too old to work but had saved up some beautiful natural crooks for sleigh runners, intending to use them in making his last sleigh before retiring. I needed a sleigh for my pair of dapple gray horses. Mr. Walker promised to make one of the best that ever came out of his workshop. He went to work, hobbling about on his one leg, chewing tobacco, and crooning. After a good long wait he showed me his masterpiece. The bunks were six feet long, and the rear and front runners were adjustable for length. The rear runners had sharp dogs to keep the sleigh from running backwards on a hill. The rack and other parts were beautifully painted. It was the work of a master craftsman.

109

Bill Leary made me promise that I would give him first chance to buy the sleigh if I ever wanted to sell. A year later I sold my horses and wagon and offered the sleigh for sale to Bill. It became his prize possession.

The Learys had a woodlot on the edge of the village where they cut firewood to sell. The road into it was narrow and required skill in handling horses and sleigh without hitting trees. One day Bill went to Carthage and did not return till night. When he saw his sleigh the next morning, he grabbed his double bitted ax and went looking for Art. He told Bessie he was going to kill him. After she had got him calmed down, she found out that Art had taken a crosscut saw and cut the bunks and rack of the sleigh down to four feet in width. Art stayed away from his father for a week or more. Bill stored the sleigh behind his barn and never used it again.

After the state had acquired the land up the river, Art took out a Conservation Department permit for a guide's camp of regulation design. He also bought himself a guide's license in accordance with a new system of registering guides throughout the Adirondacks. Wilfred had said of these licenses, "I never git one of dem cause people tink I'm a greenhorn." His reason for thinking this way was that several newcomers had bought licenses without any guiding experience. The main qualifications seemed to be the fee of two dollars and the ability to sign your name.[16] It was amusing to see some of these new licensed guides get lost along with their parties. Some of them had to be led out of the woods by their own employers.

Art located his camp a few rods off the Five Ponds Trail not far from the boat landing at Wolf Creek Spring Hole on the Oswegatchie River. He made a deal with Wilfred, who was to help him build his camp in return for permission to stay there as long as Wilfred desired. They made a framework about twelve feet by twenty-four, using dead dry tamarack poles. Art acquired some heavy, thick canvas from a paper mill and covered this material with waterproofing before he put it on the framework. It didn't work. The first rain drove them out of the camp. Art said, "I'll get five gallons of paint and stop it from leaking." Five gallons didn't go very far. Every time Art came up the river he would bring five gallons more. After this treatment the inside of the camp acquired the natural decoration of a white and pink mold. Wilfred was getting disgusted and said, "My lan! Harter has spend more for de paint dan two new tent would cost." The camp kept on leaking. Finally Art said, "I'll have to buy a paint factory or get a new waterproof canvas."

110

The canvas was cheaper than the factory, so he covered his camp with new canvas.

One day Art was guiding a fly fisherman on his first day in camp. The fisherman was anxious to have some trout for supper but was having no luck with his flies at all. Finally he suggested that Art try with a worm, so Art put on a worm and cast out. The moment the bait hit the water a large trout snapped the worm from the hook and disappeared with lightning speed. The fisherman was excited and wished he could have had such a strike as this on his fly. Being a true fly fisherman, he wouldn't try the worms. He got impatient, for Art was taking considerable time to rebait. At last the fisherman said, "What in the world is taking you so long? Get your bait back in the water." Art turned his head around facing his employer and said, "By the powers of Moll Kelly. Did you ever try picking up a night crawler and putting it on a hook with no thumb?"

Art had several men at his camp one August after they had paddled up from the Inlet House with their gear. Light rainstorms in the morning developed into a regular cloudburst in the afternoon. The Oswegatchie above Wanakena rises very rapidly during and after a heavy rain. As it got dark while the men were eating supper, Art said, "Don't let me forget to tie up the canoes after I get the dishes done." One of the men offered to go down and tie the boats. Art cautioned him to be sure and pull them up onto the bank and fasten them securely. After breakfast in the morning they all went down to the boat landing to go fishing and try their luck in high water. When they reached the river, the canoes were all standing on end in eight feet of water with their stems pointing toward the sky. The man who had tended to them had tied them without pulling them up the bank. One member of the party said, "Oh, hell, no fishing today; let's go back to camp, play cards, and drink beer." When they returned to camp, one man went to get the beer out of the little brook where they had put it to keep cool and found it was now in a raging stream several feet deep. Since the beer was more indispensable than the boats, one member of the party went in after it.

One summer Art had a party of six men who had made arrangements to stay three weeks. One of the men was very disagreeable and would not do anything the other members of the party wanted to do. After they had been in camp a few days, the party decided to go to Wolf Pond, which was a five-mile hike, and stay for a week. The disagreeable one said, "I'll stay in camp with Wilfred." Everyone was pleased except Wilfred. Before the party was ready to leave Art got him aside and told

111

him to try and get rid of the guy. Wilfred said, "Ol boy, I do dat." He thought all that day and evening trying to hit on some way to make it unpleasant for the unwelcome guest without being downright rude. About midnight he got his answer unexpectedly, for the guest woke Wilfred and asked him what was making the noises outside. Wilfred could hear the rattling of tin cans from the garbage pit. Soon an eerie, squeaking shriek penetrated the calm night. Wilfred grabbed the hedge-hog club from its peg on the wall, and with the light from his battered flashlight went out to investigate. The guest was so frightened he shivered like a leaf. He heard a couple of heavy thuds. Then Wilfred rushed into camp all out of breath and said, "Dat war a painter." The terrified guest lit the lamps and spent the rest of the night trying to read. In the morning he asked Wilfred if he would take him to Wanakena, for he said he had just remembered some important things he had forgotten to take care of at home. He left a note for his friends. I met Wilfred at the post office the day after the man departed. Wilfred told me what had happened, and added, "If dat coon come to de can dump tonight, I open a can of salmon for him."

One afternoon a few of Art's guests were sunning themselves during the hottest part of the midsummer day in the front yard of his camp. Wilfred was entertaining them with his tales of wildwood life. Suddenly one of the guests pointed and wanted to know what was coming up the trail. Wilfred squinted through the fog of Warneke Brown smoke rising from his corncob pipe and said, "Dat is a frog from de big swamp." Art had been down at the river painting one of his canoes with green paint. The black flies and punkies had been biting badly, and Art had hit at them on top of his head with the brush loaded with paint. He looked the image of what Wilfred said was coming. After the men had finished their laughter at the sight of Art, Wilfred said, "Dat is nuttin, you should see him when he dress out a deer. My lan! He look like he walk in to kick out de gut."

It got so one didn't dare leave his canoe along the river. Some sport would steal it and leave it way down the river when he was through with it. One of the new set of Wanakena guides never bought any guiding equipment and always depended on borrowing as much as he could. One day four men hired this guide to take them to Carter's Landing to fish for trout. Art had just arrived in town from his camp and had heard about this party. He could see that the guide was looking for canoes to borrow, so he told his friends he was going to hide his canoe to be sure he kept it from this sponger. Since all of his other boats were in use, he was sure they would be all right. He walked back to his camp and paddled the canoe to a point some two miles upstream from his landing. Here he dragged it back into a thicket of small evergreen trees. Since the river was very shallow at this point and the fishing was poor for several hundred rods in either direction, he was sure he had it well hidden. He walked back to town and told the men there that he felt it was worth the trip to know his canoe was where nobody would ever find it.

A few days later Art strolled into the general store to find this "borrowing" guide sitting on a brand new pack basket. His party, with torn clothes and bad tempers, had just settled their huge bill with him. Art kept looking at the pack basket the so-called guide was sitting on. Finally the guide said, "I borrowed your basket. I saw it hanging in your garage while you were away." Art's face was very red, not only because his new basket had been borrowed but because he would never sit on a pack basket and ruin it. The guide then told Art he had left his canoe at Carter's. Art roared, "By the curse of the seven snotty orphans, you never found my canoe." "Oh yes, I did," the guide yelled. "Someone had stolen it from you and hid it back in the brush." Art in-

ART AND BESSIE LEARY
Off-season, when not host at his camp upriver, Art spent quiet evenings with his sister in the parlor of the Leary Hotel in Wanakena.

(Courtesy Laura Ward)

sisted that it couldn't have been his canoe until the guide explained he
had dragged his party through the brushy, almost impassable banks of
the river trying to fish from the shore and had accidentally found the
canoe. This explained why the guests' clothes were so torn and ragged.
No one else ever tried to fish from those banks. A madder Irishman
never lived at that moment than Art, especially after the local boys kid-
ded him about hiding his canoe.

Several years after Art had opened his camp, Wilfred brought a
guest from Rochester, New York, to spend a few weeks. They paddled
up the river and started to tote their supplies and baggage from the
canoe landing at Wolf Creek Spring Hole to Art's camp. Wilfred got a
quart of moonshine out of his pack, and they sat down with other guests
outside the camp at an old wooden table. Wilfred poured out a drink
for his guest and then one for himself. After the usual salutations the
drinks were tossed off with aplomb. Wilfred left the bottle on the table
and started down the trail saying, "I will go down to de landing and tie
up de boat." While he was gone, his guest said, "I'll hide his quart and
then when he comes back we'll ask him for a drink." The guest put the
quart under an old rotten egg crate among some large bushes he found
fully a hundred feet from camp. A few minutes after Wilfred returned,
the guest said, "Wilfred, aren't you going to have another drink?" Spruc-
ing up, Wilfred replied, "Yah, I'll do dat." He started out on a perfect
line directly to where the guest had hid the bottle and then returned
without a glance toward the table. He poured out drinks for all who had
witnessed the joke that hadn't worked. After questioning him, the guests
found that years before he had hid the bottle he kept in camp in that
identical place. He went there without thinking about it at all.

Art was an exceptionally good cook and was unique in his preparation of some of the food he served. Every morning you would be served
sourdough pancakes with a perfectly fried egg on top of them. You were
not allowed in the kitchen or dining room until you were called. Sometimes only an imaginary line separated these two rooms, but the guests
well knew their limits after they were in camp a day or two. If you
weren't on time for the meal, the food went on your plate just the same
and no complaining was tolerated. His pancakes were delicious. Some
of the lady guests went so far as to call them exquisite.

One morning when the breakfast table was seated to its capacity
with men and their wives, one of the ladies said, "My, these pancakes
are light. And isn't it lovely the way he serves them with an egg?"
Wilfred shyly spoke up, saying, "Mam, do you know why Harter put de

114

egg on dem?" The lady said no, she didn't. Wilfred explained, "Mam, if you take your knife and fork and lift up de egg, you will see de panacake float away. Dat is why Harter put de egg on in de kitchen."

If Art had been guiding and making such wonderful pancakes at the time the Pancake King ran his camp at Griffin Rapids, I am afraid the Pancake King might have lost his title. Art inherited his sourdough starter from Wilfred but had added so many different ingredients that it finally contained all the known vitamins. From time to time it developed several kinds of mold. It must have contained penicillin, for no one ever had a cold while eating at Art's camp. Art always claimed one of his pancakes was as good as one antihistamine tablet. He was careful not to use up all his starter at one time, for if it ever ran out its magic formula could never be duplicated. Wilfred originally found the starter in a small Canadian village in the gold mining section of Cobalt. He had worked for a year in this section and then spent all his earnings for gold stock. I guess the sourdough starter he brought home was worth more than his gold stock. He frequently said, "I wish I had give de money to de leetle French girl dat give me de starter. Den she would alway be in de dough."

One time a guest found several frying pans behind the camp with the handles broken off. Wondering about them, he asked Wilfred how it was that so many handles had been broken. "You watch Harter tonight when he do de dish," Wilfred replied. Art had a unique way of cleaning his frying pans. That night the guest watched him come out of the kitchen with a frying pan in each hand, walk up to a spruce tree, and give the pans a terrific swing against the trunk. Presto! The grease left the pans and so did one of the handles.

It seems that without eggs Art would have had to go out of business. There was hardly a thing he baked or fried or boiled that didn't get an egg thrown in. He never allowed anyone to wash his coffee pot. When he left camp for any time, he left grounds and what liquid coffee there was right in the one-gallon pot. Upon returning to camp, he would add fresh coffee with an egg thrown in for good measure. Green, blue, black, pink, and white mold could be seen in his coffee pot most of the time, but everyone raved about the wonderful coffee he made. Perhaps the mold added to its flavor. At least, it never seemed to hurt anyone. One morning, though, Wilfred said, "Harter, you will have to dump de pot, for de coffee is so strong I have to use bot hand to dunk de doughnut."

No member of the Leary family is left in Wanakena today. Art and his sisters never married. Belle, the older sister, died in 1920, Mrs. Leary

115

in 1928, and Bill in 1930. In 1950 Wanakena lost a great character and guide, Arthur.

For a while longer Bess continued to take in guests, such as a few fishermen, hunters, and bird watchers. By this time Wanakena had become known as a bird watcher's paradise. We and our birds had always taken each other pretty much for granted, each party going about its own business. We liked to listen to them in the spring and early summer, but we didn't often see them in the dense foliage. The bird watchers changed all that. When they began coming to Wanakena in late May or early June and stared up into the trees, the birds were so surprised that they dropped whatever they were doing and came out on the tips of the branches to get a better look. It was hard to tell which were more curious, the birds or the bird watchers. This exceptional curiosity of our birds became widely known and brought even more bird watchers to Wanakena. On sunny weekends you could hear all kinds of chirping around Leary's, such as "Oh, girls, I just saw a yellow-bellied flycatcher!"

Old Bess took them all in, wondering, no doubt, what Art would say about this new type of woodsman if he were still around. She died in 1968, the last of the Learys. The old hotel is now a private residence, but few who have ever slept or eaten there can forget the warm hospitality they received, and the good food.

16. A CAPTAIN, A SCHOOLTEACHER, AN OLD WOLF HUNTER, AND A DOG

Old-timers in Wanakena remember Bob Currie well, though he left us for Florida many years ago and is undoubtedly dead by now. Everybody called him Captain Currie because of his military bearing and the army expressions he was always using in conversation. Some people doubted that he had ever been a captain, but everyone liked him and enjoyed talking to him.

Bob Currie lived about two miles from the village at Cucumber Hole, a small bay on Dead Creek Flow. At certain times of the year the trout fishing was good there. The Rich Lumber Company and later the Wanakena Company owned the land while Currie was living there and permitted him to build a small shack, where he lived the year round.

One end of the shack was partitioned off as a woodshed. The Captain kept a dozen hens in his "parlor," as he called his living room. The nests were in a row of boxes along one wall. Each morning he would reach in and pull out an egg, which was still warm when he dropped it into his frying pan. The crew of the log train claimed they could smell the rancid grease, which he used day after day, when they rolled by his camp.

Once in a while he came into town all dressed up and shaved. People said that he wore a necktie to keep his shirt from showing how far down his neck he had washed. On one of these visits, when the Captain came into the general store looking his best, a Wanakena schoolteacher happened to be there also. Though pressing forty, she was a well-preserved, good-looking girl. The sight of the Captain and the schoolmarm together in the store put an idea into the heads of some boys from the mill, and one of them was appointed to introduce the two. The Captain stammered in embarrassment, but the schoolmarm beamed from ear to ear. She was hurting pretty bad in her almost-given-up search for a man. She was overjoyed at meeting such a fine looking man, no matter how dirty he may have been beneath his necktie. Her pleasure in the meeting finally got through to the Captain, who asked her to come and visit him at his cottage on Cucumber Hole.

She went the following weekend. When she found that the cottage was only a shack, she hesitated. But getting up her nerve, she knocked on the door. When the door opened, out flew a few hens on either side of her. The Captain invited her in. If the man-hunting instinct in her body hadn't taken over, she would never have stepped across the threshold. As it was, she no sooner stepped into the Captain's parlor than she began planning how to clean up his domain. This first visit was short. The smell overcame her staying power.

The Captain met her the following week and asked her when she was going to visit him again. She promised to come out soon. For this second trip the very next weekend, she hired a couple of boys to help carry broom, mop, soap, pail, and other cleaning items besides groceries and a few cooking pots, since the Captain's supply looked beyond redemption.

Before the caravan arrived, the Captain had taken his rowboat out to visit a friend across the flow. The schoolteacher immediately took charge. She threw out the chickens and put their nest boxes in the woodshed. She scrubbed the floor, washed the windows, and hung some little curtains. The place began to look almost respectable, but the smell lingered. Lysol did not seem to neutralize it. Sleeping quarters were a puzzle too. All the Captain had was an old army cot with a dirty looking blanket.

It was late in the day when the Captain came home, quite high from a quart of whiskey he had enjoyed with his friend. As he stumbled up the trail from the flow, he was puzzled by the white curtains in the windows. The schoolteacher stayed inside in order to surprise him. As long as the whiskey was working, he was glad to see her and was very polite. But it was not long before he began to miss the chickens. When he found them in the woodshed, he said there would have to be different arrangements in the morning. Meanwhile, he pulled another old army cot out of the junk in the woodshed and placed it next to his regular one. Then he lay down and passed out, to waken only late the next morning.

His lady friend had a nice breakfast for him. This cheered him up a little, and he agreed to leave the chickens in the woodshed for the rest of the day. He also allowed her to make a few more changes. She stayed till Monday morning.

The story of her long weekend with the Captain soon got around Wanakena, and when the women heard about it they threatened to take their kids out of her class. They did not have to worry long, for the Captain came roaring into the store asking for the schoolmarm. "She wrecked my place and threw my chickens out," he said, handing over a burlap bag. "Here is her stuff. Tell her never to come to my place again."

Finally the state bought the land at Cucumber Hole and destroyed the Captain's shack. The Captain left Wanakena never to return. The schoolteacher taught in the village several years longer, but never found a man to give the burlap bag of utensils to.

Another pair, George Muir and Queenie, got along much better than the Captain and the schoolteacher. I heard the end of their story one morning in the general store when I met Wilfred. "Dey just shot Queenie," he said.

Queenie was a beautiful German shepherd dog. I had known her for the nine years of her life. No dog ever served her master more faithfully, and no master loved his dog more than George did. As I went to see what was left of her, I wondered how such a faithful servant could be treated like this. I suddenly remembered something and looked at her right front paw. Yes, there was that large deep scar which had only recently healed. The other paw showed signs of being cut from running on the spring's icy crust for many miles.

In his younger days George had been a noted wolf hunter, but now for over forty years he had been a caretaker and watchman on one of the most remote corners of a large private preserve.[17] The main camp was near a flag stop railroad station. Eight miles back in the forest was a cabin overlooking a beautiful little lake. This cabin was old George's home for his long years of service, during which he patrolled the posted lines to keep off poachers and trespassers. It was twelve miles to Wanakena, the nearest village, by the route George took.

There was a one wire telephone line which ran from the main camp to George's cabin. Sometimes the phone might ring for a long time if George was in the woods or not in the mood to answer it. It was a very lonely job, and the winters were long and cold. Nevertheless, George loved his job and dreaded a trip to the "outside," as he called it. For many years he made only one trip to the outside during the winter. During the warmer part of the year he made more frequent trips. When he was afraid that someone might trespass while he was gone, he would bake up a batch of biscuits, put out a pan of water, and leave Queenie locked up in his cabin to protect it. She might be alone for a week or more, but she left the biscuits alone and drank only a little water.

On one occasion when I was invited to the camp on Gull Lake, George related how Queenie would start eating the biscuits when she heard him approaching the camp. On this day when we arrived at camp, we could hear her greetings, though the barks were muffled because Queenie was eating biscuits. When we let her out, she ran around the cabin many times to show her welcome for her master.

One cold, clear midwinter day old George walked into my house and asked me if I would drive him to his hometown, which was some forty miles distant. He drank a cup of tea with me while Queenie had some dog biscuits and milk. The old man called my attention to one of her paws, which was badly cut, and also to her other paws, which were sore from being cut by the icy crust on the snow. They had made the trip out of the woods in twelve hours. I noticed the old man was not as strong as usual, although the snowshoeing had been good according to what he told me.

When the snow began to melt in the spring, old George arrived in town early one morning on his way back to camp. The warm weather during the previous few days had caused him much anxiety for fear that the melting snow might make travel in the woods difficult. He was not feeling well and asked Art Leary to go with him as far as Art's camp, which was over six miles along the route George used. He planned to

119

stay there all night and then, if he was able, to walk the remaining six miles the following day.

When George and Art started out in the morning, the day was a cloudy and dull one and the soft snow had frozen very hard during the night. An icy crust had formed which held them up without their snowshoes. They reached Art's camp in two hours, and by noon they had eaten a hot dinner and rested. The old man said he never felt better, so he guessed he would continue the rest of the way and take advantage of the hard crust. He was sure that he could easily reach his cabin before dark. Art boiled some eggs and made some sandwiches for George to take with him, and George borrowed a small double-bitted ax. They wished each other farewell, and each left for his own destination.

Old George had promised his employer that he would either telephone the main camp or make a trip over to it so the family would know he had arrived safely. He was eighty years old at this time, and his fading ability caused the family to worry about him.

No word came from the old man, and it was several days before a telephone connection could be made between Wanakena and the main camp to inquire about him. The main camp sent a man over to see about George. This man returned with the news that no one had been at George's cabin for a long while. When this news was relayed to Wanakena, a search party was immediately organized.

Since Wilfred was the only person who knew the exact way George would travel on the last six miles of his trip, he led the party. George had never made a trail, for he didn't want anyone to find his camp. By this time all the snow had melted, so it was not possible to do any tracking; the tracks would have been long gone anyway. The swamps were full of water and the streams were at flood height. Wilfred led along the probable route and had some men walking with him off to the sides. Several trips were made, and each time the covered territory was extended a bit further. It was agreed that shot signals would be used if anything was found.

On the third day one of the men heard a dog bark and spied the ends of a pair of snowshoes. He ran closer and found the snowshoes leaning against a tree. He announced his discovery by use of the agreed shot signals and then advanced quickly to find out what he could. As he looked over a fallen tree, he was met with a savage roar. There was Queenie guarding the body of her dead master. She couldn't understand all those shots and how friends could make such an alarming noise. Then people came from all directions. She felt she must keep them

120

away. Suddenly she heard a familiar voice, and when Wilfred called, "Queenie," she greeted him with cheerful barks and a wagging tail. The searchers found that her paws had been cut, for she had made many trips to camp and back trying to get help yet afraid to leave her master alone.

Queenie was in bad shape after her long watch. A relative of George in another village was phoned. He did not want Queenie. He gave orders to shoot her.

17. A GUIDE'S HUNTING CAMP

About a year after I had returned to Wanakena from service in World War I, I decided to get a Conservation Department permit for a permanent tent platform and build a camp on some ideal spot along the banks of the Oswegatchie River, which I loved so much. I wanted to be upriver from the Inlet House a considerable distance and started a long search for my ideal spot. I found a small creek flowing into the river from the north halfway between Round Hill Rapids and Crooked Rapids, approximately a quarter mile below Carter's Landing. The stream was called Carlson's Creek after the Carlson who built a short railroad spur along its bank for hauling out logs years ago. At this spot the road is about 500 feet north of where I planned to build the camp.

The woods around the site consisted of tamarack, white pine, balsam, spruce, hemlock, and a few large birch trees. The tamaracks were plentiful and ranged in size from two to thirty inches in diameter. Saw flies had visited this section some years before and killed a large number of the tamaracks. The dead trees stood like flagpoles. Only a short section at their butts had started to rot, so they were easy to fell by accidentally backing into them. The cutting of standing trees, green or dead, is prohibited in state forest preserve land.

I had a friend of several years standing, Clarence Phillips, who had spent his boyhood days in Lewis County and had done a hitch in the United States Cavalry. He was a natural woodsman, an excellent guide, and a very good hunter. I asked him if he would like to go in with me

121

in setting up a hunting and fishing camp, and he readily agreed. I was pleased to have him as partner, for he was a good man in the woods.

We started the camp by laying out a building 12 by 28 feet with a partition which separated it into two rooms. One room was for the kitchen and the other was to be the dining room. The construction started with a base of logs about 10 inches in diameter built up three logs high. On the top log we stood poles about 5 inches in diameter to make the sides 6 feet high. On top of these poles a pole plate was nailed all around. On the center of each end pole plate a 6-inch pole 4 feet long was nailed upright to support the 28-foot ridgepole. Approximately 3-inch pole rafters were made and placed about 18 inches apart with the ends beveled off to fit the pole plates and fit even with the sides. Eight-inch logs were placed on the ground between the sides to form the floor joists. These were leveled off to make an even base for the floor. A door was cut in the logs on one end and a door frame, made of poles, installed. A screen door was put in this frame and a piece of canvas hung at the top of the frame so it could be rolled down in cold weather. A window and a screen were installed on the kitchen end and another in the dining room.

The completed frame was measured for a waterproof canvas which would cover the roof and extend down the sides to the base logs. We sent to Sears Roebuck for the canvas and ordered it with eyelets spaced two feet apart so it could be tied in place with ropes. The ropes would give to allow the canvas to shrink and expand with the weather.

The floor was made of matched white pine boards which were painted with gray floor paint. A large old-fashioned wood-burning cook stove with a water reservoir on one end was installed to furnish plenty of heat in cold weather. It had an oven of ample size for baking. Tables and benches were built, and then the kitchen and dining room dishes were brought in.

Diagonally across from the front of the kitchen and dining room, at a distance of about 30 feet, the sleeping camp was built. This building was 14 by 32 feet and of the same construction as the smaller camp. Ten double bunks were built and fitted with springs and mattresses. A large wood stove was placed at the center of the camp and to one side. A long table and benches were placed opposite the stove. An open front, lean-to washstand was built to one side of the front of the sleeping camp. A V-shaped trough carried the waste water to a deep hole behind the stand. Outdoor rustic seats were constructed and a rack to hold firewood. A short distance from the camp a deep hole was dug for the garbage pit. Clarence and I had a discussion as to what type of out-house to build. Should it be rustic or should we send to a mail order house and get a modern one? We finally decided to keep everything as woodsy as possible.

When the camp was completed, we took a few days to rest up after the strenuous work we had done. Cutting the logs and poles was hard work. Peeling the bark from the tamarack poles was slow and tedious, for the poles had dried and the bark was stuck fast. We had to peel the bark off to prevent wet rot and prevent insects eating the wood.

The Conservation Department rules stated that the camp had to be occupied or visited twice a month in winter and once every forty-eight hours the rest of the year. There were several other camps of this type located nearby, so during the winter we took turns looking at each other's camps and scraping the snow from the roofs. Generally, it required an overnight stop if the snowshoeing was bad going, which it often was.

We dug a root cellar into the side of a sandy knoll near the camp and lined it with poles. It never froze in the winter, and we were able to keep vegetables and canned goods in good shape for our guests and ourselves as well.

Most of my memories of the camp I shared with Clarence are of days of fun and days of hard but agreeable work. The sharpest memory, how-ever, is of a day of bad luck and the hardest work I ever put in. It was in the latter part of April. A long North Country winter was slowly breaking up, and Clarence and I were eager to go upriver again and to get our muskrat traps set as early as possible. A cold night had put a heavy crust over the remaining snowy spots on the road from Lonesome Pond (now Sunny Pond) to Inlet. The road had not been plowed out that winter because no one had been staying at the Inlet House. A thaw before the cold snap had opened the river above Inlet as far as we could see on a reconnoitering hike up the Rapids Trail.

We put our boat, motor, traps, and groceries on my truck and at five in the morning left for Inlet. We had no trouble on the frozen road until we reached the top of the hill just above the footbridge. We did not dare take a chance on going down the hill on the crust, so we un-loaded the boat, put all our trappings in it, and left it until our return by trail. As I turned the truck around, it broke through the crust into about twenty inches of snow. After a great deal of shoveling, we got the truck on solid crust again and started back to Wanakena. We did not want to leave the vehicle at Inlet, where it might have been stranded by thaw or more snow.

We reached Wanakena at 7:00 A.M., had some coffee and toast, and at 7:30 left for Inlet on the trail. The south-facing riverbank was mostly bare for the first mile. Then we came to an ice jam on the river which backed the water up at a low spot. For the next half mile we waded through snow and ice water to get back on the trail.

We finally arrived at the boat we had left on the hill. We skidded it down the road into the river, put the motor on, and shoved off. Just as we were getting under way, a large cake of ice came at us. The current was fast and the ice cake reached from shore to shore. We hurriedly got the boat ashore and dragged it to a spot that the ice could not hit. Once the cake had passed by, we started again. No more ice appeared for the next two miles, and made good time. We found a couple of trapping logs, wired them to the alders, and set two traps in the notches we cut. Each year the notches appear at a different angle. After drying out during the summer, the logs never float the same way the following year.

During the next few miles we encountered more ice, some from shore to shore. The packs did not seem to be very long, and we got out on the ice and pulled the boat along until we came to open water again. We reached Griffin Rapids about noon and stopped there for lunch.

After resting till one o'clock, we started upriver again. The going was good for a couple of miles, and then we struck a place where we could neither float the boat nor drag it on the ice. The ice had settled near the bottom, and water six inches deep was flowing over it. We decided to go ashore, tie up the boat, and walk across the swamp to the old railroad grade (which is now the fire truck road). The walking was good for a few rods, but then we began to break through the snow into ice water up to our knees.

It was getting dark fast, and we were just about paralyzed with the cold. At one time we thought we would never make it. But soon we could see a long white ribbon ahead of us. We knew it to be the railroad grade, where snow had drifted along the side. In a few more agonizing rods we left the swamp and at last were on the road.

We took off our shoes and wrung the water out of our socks. The road was bare for the next mile, and in spite of its being pitch black, our spirits rose. In another mile they sank again, for the road ahead was covered with about a foot of snow. We sank to the ground with each step. Only now and then did we hit a bare spot. We had our packs, but now discovered we had forgotten to put any food in them except one loaf of bread.

After traveling what seemed hours, we came to the junction where

124

our trail to camp left the railroad grade. It was a good thing we had lots of matches, for from now on we waddled ahead by match light, our flashlight being in the boat in a box of groceries. The snow was deeper on the trail through the thick evergreens, and again we talked about never being able to make the camp. We rested a few minutes and then started with more courage. With about our last strength gone, we saw the camp a few feet ahead. A more welcome sight I have never had.

We stumbled in after shoveling the snow away from the door. Clarence said, "Light the lantern and lamps so we can see to build a fire." I now discovered that someone had been in camp and used up every drop of kerosene in the lamps and lantern and also the dry wood we always left. A short distance from the camp we kept our reserve supply of kerosene between some large boulders that could not be easily seen from the camp trail. By more match light we reached the oil cans only to find six inches of ice over them. By hacking with our knives, we finally got a two-gallon can loose. When the lantern and lamps were lighted, Clarence got out the bucksaw. We dug some poles out of the snow that we had put there to cut up. Only the thought that we might eventually get warm gave us the energy to saw up some wood. At last we carried an armful of stove wood into the camp and loaded up the stove. Clarence gave the wood a shot of "Daniel Boone" fire starter, and I touched it off with a match.

Soon the smoke was so dense that we could not stay in the camp. The stovepipe went through a hole in a large piece of tin nailed to the framework. Instead of an elbow, just outside we had a T joint so we could take a cap off and clean the pipe out. The cap was rusted, and we now had to pound it off with a hammer. It finally came loose, and so did the pipe on the stove. Flames almost set the roof afire. We grabbed a large dishpan and threw it over the opening on the stove outlet. Now we discovered that squirrels had built a nest in the pipe. After cleaning the nest out, we assembled the outside pipe and then tackled the big job of fitting the inside pipe on the stove with flames shooting up. By wrapping rags and towels over our gloves and with a little luck, we finally got the pipe together. Smoke once again filled the cabin. Choking, we rushed to open the door and window. When we could see each other through the thinning smoke and a little warmth began to creep into our bones, we had just strength enough left to set the alarm before rolling off to sleep in our bunks, supperless.

The alarm went off at 1:00 A.M. I had to be at Wanakena at 8:00 A.M. to carry the mail and to make arrangements for my substitute to

125

take over for the next two weeks. I had some hot coffee and half of the loaf of bread—the only food we had in camp. I waited almost an hour before the feeling came back into my feet, and then started out on the trail to Wanakena with the lantern.

During the night the river rose and washed out the remaining ice. Clarence took our canoe and paddled to the place where we had left the boat. When I got back to camp, he was there with the boat and the food. I was glad to get a warm meal after the twelve-mile hike.

The next day we towed the canoe to High Falls, carried it around the falls, and paddled to Beaverdam, setting traps along the way. We then walked back to High Falls and took the boat with motor back to camp. The next morning we set traps down the river to a couple of miles above Inlet and then came back to camp. The following morning we went to High Falls in the big boat, walked to Beaverdam, and then paddled back to High Falls, picking up a muskrat once in a while. This daily routine went on for two weeks until we pulled all our traps. We then took our hides to Gouverneur and sold them for $1.50 each.

When we got home, we sat down and figured out that the rats had cost us about $12 apiece. That was the end of our rat trapping on the Oswegatchie.

During the fishing and hunting seasons business at our camp was good for several years. Many of our guests got into the habit of coming back year after year, and we enjoyed this association with cheerful men, and sometimes their wives, on vacation. Our mutual friend Wilfred had helped us build the camp and, once it was completed, helped entertain our guests with his many colorful stories. By this time he was too old for much active guiding, but it was always a pleasure to have him around. During the 1930s, however, business began to drop off. There were many reasons for this.[18] One was certainly the depression, which caused people to give up their vacations or skimp on them. Another was the fact that fishing was getting poorer along the upper Oswegatchie. Also, the newly completed roads in the area brought in a different class of people. The Civilian Conservation Corps was established and built a gravel road over the old railroad bed from Wanakena, first to Carter's Plains and then on to High Falls. This road was closed to the public and was supposedly used only by Conservation Department employees. Our camp was only a few hundred yards from the road, and the sound and sight of the trucks and cars took away the feeling of being in the backwoods away from everything. The tramping of many feet around our camp had worn the topsoil down until in wet weather the black

126

mud was slimy and slippery. We tried to keep this area covered with pine needles to prevent such a mess and spent lots of time collecting and spreading them around the camp. One time after we had just finished doing such a job, we left to go to Wanakena for the weekend. It was between fishing and hunting seasons and there were no guests in the camp. When we returned, we found three women and their husbands occupying the camp. The women greeted us with "See how nicely we have cleaned up the yard." They had raked up all the needles and dumped them over the bank.

We asked this party to move on, for we discovered they had also used up almost a cord of wood we had cut, eaten some of our groceries, and used other items belonging to the camp. Our request started a big argument. They claimed they had a right to use the camp since it was on state-owned land. Eventually they did move on, but this sort of thing began to happen more and more frequently. "River rats," as we called them, were stealing supplies from all the camps along the river, and several fires were started by their carelessness. At that time there were only two fire wardens or rangers to take care of the whole section. The guides all pitched in and helped these men keep the trails clean and put out any fires they could.

In 1940 we decided to tear our camp down and move out. Between the camp and the river was an open meadow. We rolled and carried all the logs and poles down there and made a large pile of them. That night it rained and we made a big fire of all our work. The next day we spent carrying water to extinguish the hot bed of coals, and that afternoon we moved our salvageable supplies down the river by boat. Only memories remained of the good times we had had in our camp on the banks of the Oswegatchie.

18. SPORTS AND ENGINEERS

Up until 1917 only a few automobiles had been able to get to Wanakena from Benson Mines over the rugged dirt road, and then only when the road was perfectly dry. This year was the one which saw Wanakena and its peace and quiet fall to the pantywaist woodsman. The Wanakena Company had to make a tough decision. The price of steel was so high that they were offered more for their railroad rails than they had paid

127

for them new. The company reluctantly sold the rails and all remaining railroad equipment. During the fall of 1917 the rails were taken up and the roadbed made into an automobile road. The Hotel Wanakena started down the trail into a land of memories, as most of the famous old Adirondack hotels did as soon as easy transportation facilities were developed and vacationers became more mobile.

God bless the souls of the honest, rugged people that loved the beautiful wilderness so much that they were willing to ride a stagecoach from Potsdam to a magnificent hotel built on a rise of ground overlooking charming Massawepie Lake, a few miles northeast of Cranberry Lake. This hotel accommodated over three hundred guests and was full all summer. Think how much these grand people must have loved the solitude and wilderness to have ridden over forty miles by stagecoach from the nearest railroad. The building of the railroad through Childwold and Piercefield, about ten miles away, brought civilization too close, and this beautiful hotel soon closed down forever. For many years after it closed it was kept in repair as a sort of memento by a new owner. After the death of this owner in 1947, the building was razed; it had stood unused for over a quarter of a century.[19]

The six miles of new road built on the old railroad grade from Wanakena to Benson Mines was one road where there was no speeding. The many fills were narrow, and the big fill over the old trestle had most people holding their breath until the cut on either end was safely reached. Such conditions were the concern of the different proprietors that ran the hotel at Wanakena, and each hoped that someday there would be a better road to make better business. They were wrong in their desires as they found out later when a hard-surfaced road was built to Wanakena. Business dropped off at an alarming rate, and the Hotel Wanakena closed its doors shortly after the end of World War II. It had survived longer than many Adirondack hotels.

The struggling automobiles that conquered the muddy and rocky roads into the deep Adirondacks brought in a far different type of person from the ones who had come by train and horse. The newcomers called themselves "sports." I could see that nothing around here was going to have even a sporting chance to survive the new influx unspoiled. I figured it was time to find out the real meaning of the word "sport," so I looked up the definition in the dictionary. One of the definitions I found was "an animal or plant of abnormal constitution." Now I wanted to find out about the word "constitution" and found that the same dictionary defined it as "body strength." I wanted to be sure of my

128

research, so I looked up "strength" and found it meant "power of endurance." When these data were assembled and applied to one of the sports I knew, they showed what I had expected, which was that nothing was mentioned of "brains." Summing up, it appears that a sport is an animal with no brains, an abnormal constitution, body strength, and power of endurance.

Right now I want to take time out and apologize to all good woodsmen and nature lovers who in the past I might have erroneously called "sports."

During the many years I have followed the improved roads into the Adirondacks, I have observed these latter-day sports and would like to show you how they work. Take a ride with me in my car and let's look at some roadside scenes. We are on a nice dirt road just wide enough for one car, and to our left are a cottage and several cabins facing the river. See how neat the yards about the buildings are kept, for they are privately owned. To our right the woods are owned by the State of New York, whose property borders the edge of the road. Look. The sports have had the body strength to lug in and dump cans, bottles, paper, and every kind of garbage along this mile or more of publicly owned property. See the holes in that birdhouse. Some sport with an abnormal constitution put them there with a gun while trying to shoot a bird the property owner had tried to attract and feed. That old piece of paper tacked on that tree? Some sport with the power of endurance shot at it for a target, not caring what might be behind the tree.

Now we are driving on the concrete road called the Oswegatchie Trail, where enough blood has been drained from the battered, crushed, and broken bodies of the people killed by the automobiles on the mad holiday rush through the Adirondacks to paint the white strip red from here to there. The Bloody Oswegatchie Trail. Once a path of quiet and solitude wending its rugged but peaceful way through the great trees and green swamps.

Let's stop and have a drink in this hotel by the road. Oh, look at that 250-pound lady sport with her skinny boy friend. "How much are your double bedrooms per night?" she bellows, and then, "Are the springs modern?" I guess she does wear the pants even if she ain't got 'em on today. When the proprietor tells her what the rates are and assures her the springs are modern, she squawks, "I want to see if your beds are clean." The proprietor can't get used to people of this type, and his face flushes as he tells her he would be glad to show her the room. This sport has the power of endurance to waddle up the winding stairway and tear

129

the clothes off the beds to see if they are clean. After she has wiggled her big butt back down the stairs, she tells the proprietor that there is a tourist camp back down the road where she can stay for fifty cents less for the night. When she has gone, the proprietor sends the maid up to repair the beds and remarks that this sort of thing is happening more often each day. When the insulting questions become unbearable, he just tells the sports he has no rooms available.

We continue on our way and stop at a gas station on the Oswegatchie Trail. My friend says he would like to use the rest room while I get gasoline, but he soon comes back saying it is locked up for repairs. The station attendant gives him the key and mentions that he allows only people he knows to use it, for the general traveling public act like a bunch of hogs when they enter such a place. We stop at a roadside stand to get some hot dogs and listen as a farmer tourist tells how a sport has shot holes in his beehives and torn down his fences. During the hunting season he has had to stop work and patrol his property.

Now let's go back and see how these sports operate in the forest. We really have a tough time now, but let's try.

Several years before improved roads and automobiles reached Wanakena, a few intelligent engineers appeared in the wild virgin forests in the northern part of Herkimer County. These gentlemen and their wives arrived dressed in fur coats, and their kind, gentle faces were admired by all the native animals of the section. Even the speckled brook trout looked up through the sparkling water of their home and admired them. (For a while, in their selfishness, even the sports liked them.) These gentlemen had lots of intelligence. In addition they had strong legs, a wide flat tail, and tireless energy. They were harmless to all other living creatures. (Keep quiet, deer hunters, I'll take care of you later.) These gracious denizens of the wildwoods were very happy to be back in the Adirondacks, where they had been exterminated years before by greedy trappers.

Once reestablished in the Adirondacks, the beaver soon spread into the region of the upper Oswegatchie. Only three generations are allowed in a beaver colony. The two-year-olds are forced to become wanderers and to build dams and houses of their own in another part of the woods. During pregnancy each year the mother beaver probably gets edgy with the prospect of another litter to nurse. So she kicks out the two-year-olds, which up to this time have required a lot of attention. The change in her disposition must be a shock to the outcasts. A few of them never seem to recover. Once in a while there is a lazy or neurotic

130

BEAVERDAM, UPPER OSWEGATCHIE

This beaver house at the headwaters of the East Branch is 100 feet in circumference. The pond backed up by the dam was a celebrated fishing hole in the 1920s.

beaver that won't work in harmony with others. He roams the streams looking for food and burrows into a bank for protection. He is called a tramp or bank beaver. But the majority of the two-year-olds, after a little student engineering on play dams on tiny streams, go out and build new workable dams and houses on their own. Sometimes they allow a wise old muskrat to live with them as sentinel. He watches the pond for danger so the beaver can devote all their time to their construction.

When a family of these brothers and sisters, joined by others, reached the headwaters of the East Branch of the Oswegatchie, they pitched in on a really big engineering project. At this point the river funnels out into tiny spring brooks, some of which are only a few hundred feet long from where they emerge from under higher land. The beavers worked long and hard hours and soon had a dam about three hundred feet long and eight feet high. It made a pond of considerable size and depth. This pond also contained their house, which was over a man's head in height and had a circumference of about one hundred feet. A high knoll rose from one side of the pond and was thickly covered with poplar trees, which furnished ample food for this rapidly increasing colony.

The beaver pond was fed by so many cold springs that it was a wonderful place for trout. Trout spawned there. The pond became known as Beaverdam and was noted for its excellent trout fishing. Using flies, one could catch his limit in just a few minutes. As time went on, the beaver built many more dams across the river from Beaverdam clear down to High Falls.

To reach Beaverdam, it was necessary to walk over the High Falls trail from Wanakena, a distance of about ten miles, or to paddle from the Inlet House, a distance of nearly thirty miles. The dams built by the beaver didn't spread the river out in area but did make the water deeper and thus cooler. The trouble of having to pull your canoe over dams was thus offset by the good paddling in deep water.

Eventually, the whole river from High Falls to Beaverdam became a fisherman's paradise. Its fame grew and was widely advertised. Some of the sports with body strength and power of endurance walked, in one day, the twenty mile round trip from Wanakena and returned with their limit-plus. Once, during this short-lived fish catching opportunity, a party of fourteen sports stopped at Wanakena, hired a guide, and then went on to High Falls. At High Falls they put up a tent fly in front of one of the open camps and got ready for the great kill. The next day the guide led them up the well-beaten trail to Beaverdam, and when they returned to High Falls at night each sport had his limit, all well over the legal length. Every day was the same for the two weeks of their vacation. They had the power and strength and endurance to catch fourteen baskets of trout a day for two weeks, but none had the brains to quit when one or two baskets would have been all they could have eaten. Later, behind their camp, we found a large hole dug where they had buried all the excess trout. The guide had been dismissed as soon as he had shown them the way to Beaverdam, even though he had been hired for a two-week job. He was happy he had been dismissed when he found the way they operated. Many other parties of sports operated in just such a way. In a few short years the beaver were nearly trapped out, their houses destroyed, and the dams torn out of the river by the outboard sports. The fish catching deteriorated at an alarming rate. One day we saw four young fellows, in shorts, paddling around above High Falls. They stayed all summer. They told us they had been hired by the State Conservation Department to determine why the fishing was getting so poor above High Falls. We later heard that these so-called fish biologists had reported that the trout had interbred so badly that they were running out.

The traffic became so heavy on the river that some of the sports didn't have time to walk to the toilets the state had provided and used the open camps instead. Some of the sports went into illegal trapping of beaver and even left beaver carcasses in the open camps to rot and stink. One day the district warden reported these conditions, adding that the camps were unlivable and a liability. They were burned down. Thus, for a time, the real woodsmen had no place to stay overnight.

The sports had the body strength to cut some large green spruce trees at High Falls for firewood but didn't have quite enough power of endurance to make them burn. At Carter's Landing campsite the sports climbed up some of the tall virgin white pine and cut off branches for use as bedding. They had the power of endurance to lie on these large rough boughs and look at the sickly sight they had made of the once beautiful pines. One day we stopped at Moses' Rock Spring, near Carter's, to get a jug of water and found that five sports who were camping near there had washed their dirty dishes and clothes in this clear, cold spring and had left the bottom of it filled with garbage, even though it was only two rods to the river. The alders on the banks of the river near some of the famous spring holes were cut down by these sports so they could more easily reach these spots to fish. One sport had the power of endurance to walk ten miles into the virgin forest and then build a fire to warm his can of beans on the roots of a tall dead white pine. It took three men a week to put the fire out where it had burned into the duff and spread for a hundred rods along the top of a knoll. The large pine had to be felled to extinguish the fire, and if it hadn't rained the taxpayers of this area would have had a much higher tax to pay. Local people have to pay a large percentage of the cost of fighting forest fires in their area while the sports pay nothing directly.

Now that these sports can drive easily to places that were once remote, the yearly damage they do in their mad effort to kill game would take a big book to relate. One afternoon during the hunting season two young sports without brains or experience were crossing the river on a narrow log bridge just a few rods above High Falls. When they safely reached the south shore, they loaded their guns, left the safety in fire position, and started down the trail ready for anything that dared to move in or out of their sight. One walked directly behind the other as they proceeded down a narrow trail. They jerked up their rifles to the ready at every sound of the wind, flutter of a bird, crack of a twig, or imagined sound, their fingers on the trigger ready to squeeze. Bang! The calm mountain air is set into reverberation by a high powered rifle shot. One of the men back at camp smiled and said, "I wonder if they got one so close to camp?" Yes, they had got one all right—a hunting companion right through the leg above the knee. Blood spurted dangerously fast from the wound as the men from camp arrived at the scene after hearing calls for help. It was lucky the accident occurred so close to camp where help was near. After they had carried the unfortunate victim to camp, they applied first aid and did everything they could do without professional knowledge.

Two of the men from the party ran the six miles to Wanakena for a doctor. No doctor would leave his practice to walk six miles into the woods. The nearest doctor was some nine miles from Wanakena, and the next nearest thirty-five miles. The former was consulted. He gave instructions on what to do and how to get the suffering man out of the woods. The party had paddled the twenty-one miles to High Falls. The man would have to be taken out by canoe with as little delay as possible. None of the hunters were experienced enough to paddle down the river at night, especially as the water was rising from the heavy rain which was falling. They would have tipped over in the swift rapids, and the wounded man would have been helpless and perhaps would have drowned.

When the two men returned from seeing the doctor, they came into the general store at Wanakena frantically seeking advice as to how they could get their friend out of the woods. Just at this moment Wilfred came into the store after delivering a telegram to some hunters camped three miles beyond High Falls. When he heard their story, he immediately offered to walk to High Falls and paddle the injured man down to the Inlet House. He said, "I will git him dere as safe as if he were in his mudder arm." He didn't wait for supper or a cup of coffee. Soaking wet, tired and hungry from his previous eighteen-mile walk, he led the two men back to High Falls faster than they really wanted to go. He had not guided in several years and was not so spry as in the old days, but he still amazed the young men with his rapid pace.

The wounded man was given some pills to relieve his pain and then placed in a canoe which the men carried directly to camp. The canoe with the patient was gently carried to the foot of High Falls, and Wilfred climbed in and slowly eased it out into the river. He was told to loosen the tourniquet every twenty minutes. Before he had covered the first mile, he noticed that the man was asleep. A cold, nasty rain was

134

falling and the night was pitch black. Here was a real test of Wilfred's forty years of paddling on this crooked river. When he came to the most dangerous rapids, he used a paddle in each hand, thus holding the canoe as he let it slowly drift along by the treacherous rocks. While in Wanakena, the hunters had telephoned a city for an ambulance to meet the canoe at the Inlet House. Wilfred knew this and kept repeating to himself as he struggled along, "I hope dey will be dere when we reach de end." He faithfully loosened the tourniquet as instructed but worried most that the patient would try to sit up while under the influence of the drugs he had been given. After what must have seemed like many, many hours, the young man groaned and asked, "Will we ever reach the hotel?" Just then Wilfred could see the outline of the horse barn through the first dim light of the breaking dawn and said, "Ol buck, we are dere now, you'll be safe."

WILFRED MORRISON
This is the way Wilfred looked about the time he paddled the wounded hunter down the Oswegatchie at night in a rainstorm. He is seated on a saw-buck behind the Leary Hotel.
(*Courtesy Thelma Ritz*)

The patient was carefully placed in the waiting ambulance and in a few more hours was on the operating table. When he came out of the anesthetic, he was told that the surgeon had had to take off his leg above the knee. His first words were, "I owe my life to that guide who brought me down the river." This young man was more fortunate than some who came to hunt deer and were brought back down the same river with no blood left in their bodies. Victims of the sports' power of endurance and lack of brains. Wilfred was forgotten in the excitement of getting the young man in the ambulance, and since no one thought to give him a ride to Wanakena, he walked the two miles down the trail. He didn't complain, for he understood. He was happy for having been able to help save a man's life. It made the skill of his profession really worthwhile. When he arrived at Wanakena, the clock showed it was 10:00 A.M., as it was the day before when he had left to deliver the telegram. Twenty-six miles of walking, a twenty-one-mile paddle in the dark and freezing rain, one cup of coffee, a sandwich, and one human life saved, all in twenty-four hours. Not bad for a wonderful old man in the last dim years of his life.

A Wanakena restaurant proprietor was not so fortunate. He lost not only his leg but his life when a brainless sport dropped a high-powered rifle. The gun discharged and the bullet killed the man as he was cranking his motorboat engine in order to take the sport down the river. Of course the sport said he didn't know the gun was loaded.

It would be hard to determine the exact year or period of years when the big change took place in increased game law violations and in the functions of the game protector, who has tended to become not so much a protector as a collector of dead game. Why has this shift taken place? It seems to me that the reason is that the Conservation Department[20] expects one warden to cover the same area he did before the automobile brought so many more hunters into the woods. Today so much illegal killing and trapping is done along the highways that the warden doesn't have time to get back in the woods at all. Now he has only time to collect the dead game as the violators bring it out. It seems that there should be enough men hired so that two of them could work together checking in the woods itself and working with a game collector on the highways. A protector's job is a tough one and he gets little cooperation as he tries to protect our wildlife. When a bad and continuous violation is reported as occurring in some remote part of the woods, the warden has to ask help from either the State Troopers, who also are spread very thin, or from a warden in another section.

136

Not long ago it was reported that a large party of sports in a remote section of Herkimer County was slaughtering fish and game beyond any reasonable respect for the rights of others. The officers walked into their camp unexpectedly one day before deer season opened and were shocked with what they found. The sports were just sitting down to dinner. One was cooking fresh-caught brook trout, though the season was closed. A pan of venison steak was frying on the stove, and the steaks had been cut from the ham of a doe hanging behind the camp in plain sight. Two beaver skins were on stretchers, and a man was caught skinning out a third beaver. Several muskrat skins were drying on their racks. All of this game was in violation of license regulations. Green spruce trees had been cut and used for the framework of the party's camp. The men were brought out and fined a few dollars, only to return to the woods to catch more fur to pay their fines. If there were more game protectors around to circulate in the woods, men like these wouldn't dare to flout the law so flagrantly.

The gentle beaver became the most hated creatures in the entire Adirondacks, both by the sport hunters and the sport fishermen. Each blamed the beaver for the poor fishing and the poor hunting, for they reasoned there had to be a reason other than their own actions. The hunters claimed that the beaver flooded the low lands where the deer used to yard up in heavy winters, so that the deer died from lack of food. The fishermen claimed that, by flooding the ponds, streams, and rivers, the beaver were killing the brook trout and also many trees whose roots were drowned.[21] The outboard motor boys hated the dams which obstructed navigation.

The Conservation Department got so many letters from these beaver haters that they decided to look into the matter. They sent a man to Cranberry Lake village to get some firsthand reports from the natives, the sports, and the rocking chair nature lovers, whose numbers by this time had increased so much that they had formed a club. A large gathering assembled to tell the fish expert what they thought they knew. I guess some of the sports thought there might be trouble at the crossroads, for they appeared wearing guns strapped on their belts and big sombreros. These men looked at the Conservation Department representative as if they thought he was personally to blame for all their hunting and fishing troubles. When he had been properly introduced, his first question was, "Do you think the beaver hurt . . ." His question was drowned in the uproar of voices, everyone yelling and crowding closer to the speaker. I believe he was concerned about his own safety

137

at this point. After about five minutes of this the mob was quieted down by the local warden and some other responsible men of the community. The speaker cleared his throat and started to repeat the question, but the roar started all over again, louder and longer. He finally got out his question, "Do you think the beaver hurt the trout fishing in all instances?" and sat down. The arguments flew. No one could hear the answers he attempted to give as he picked a question at random to answer from the many being asked all at once. He finally gave up in disgust and went back to Albany without any of the sage wisdom he had expected to gather.

This great hate for the beaver still exists. But I believe there are enough real wildlife devotees around to keep these animals from being exterminated.

In the middle 1930s another blow was given to wildlife by the three C's—the Civilian Conservation Corps. They were young men of army age and material, bossed by political appointees. Their main role was reforestation. You can believe they did the job if you want to, but someone else will have to tell you of the good they did. I don't know of any that they can take credit for. Some of the small streams still had some brook trout in them in spite of the onrush of the sports, for they were full of old logs, alders, and such stuff as nature had provided for shade and shelter. The banks of such streams were almost inaccessible to fishermen, so the CCC cut trails along the banks, cleaned out all the logs and shelter, and made dams to aerate the water, for, according to some experts, the trout were almost suffocating. Now the long-legged great blue heron and the sports had no trouble wading up and down these brooks, and soon there were no trout to worry about. Restocking would last only a few weeks.

Many ponds which were remote and hard to find had trout in them because it required a little work to get to them. Again the CCC made wide paths and nailed up tree markers so that the trout didn't last long here either. Many of the old trails were covered with packed leaves and needles and were fairly dry to walk on even in the rainy fall and spring. But the CCC boys dug all this out so that the first little rain turned the trails into miniature Erie Canals. The dirt they dug up was evenly divided on each side so that it was impossible to walk beside the old trail. Gravel roads were built into the forest. These were supposed to be closed to motor vehicles except for Conservation Department employees, but it was astounding how many employees the department had that had business on these roads, especially if they led to a place which had

138

good fishing or hunting. It seemed that there had never been so many forest fires as when the CCC was scattered through the forests of our land. When the organization was finally disbanded, thousands of people breathed a sigh of relief and ceased to worry so much as to what was being done to their beloved wild country.

19. HIGH LIFE

Compared to the northwestern half of St. Lawrence County, our southeastern half is definitely backwoods. That is holstein country, sloping down to the St. Lawrence. This is whitetail, beaver, and tall pine country. We don't pretend to be as civilized as our neighbors on the north, who used to turn the tables on city people downstate by calling our part of the county the South Woods and claiming it as their playground. They had (and still do have) a rock at South Colton called Sunday Rock. It was supposed to divide the civilized part of the county from the wilds. According to them, there was no law and not much religion south of Sunday Rock. Once you passed the big boulder headed south, you could do as you pleased. And they did.

But civilization has made some inroads at Wanakena and hereabouts. For sixty years now we have had the Ranger School faculty and their wives. In the days of the Rich Lumber Company we had prohibition before the country as a whole got it. Then there was the Hotel Wanakena with its veranda sitters, especially in the days of Billy Bean. Over in Benson Mines there was Sylvester (Sam) Spain, proprietor of the Ellsworth Hotel.

By bringing in Bob Fitzsimmons, Sam Spain tamed the lumberjacks for a month or two. The table he served at the Ellsworth was also a civilizing influence. He became known as the best chef in northern New York. On Sundays people from Watertown and Carthage, where they had restaurants of their own, would get on the C & A train that arrived at Benson Mines around ten in the morning, have one of Sam's great dinners, and return home by the late afternoon train.

Sam also brought capitalism in. Aside from the lumber barons, who came and went, Sam was about the first resident of our area to own

139

common stock. It came about through a salesman who registered at the Ellsworth Hotel and brought in a large trunk. He opened the trunk and took out a splendid rocking horse decorated with fancy colors and tassels. Sam, who was a great horse lover and horseman, wanted to buy it, but the salesman said it was only a sample and was not for sale. Instead he offered a set of stock certificates in the company that made the rocking horses in a city several hundred miles away. Sam bought about a thousand dollars' worth of shares. Some time later he got notice that the company was about to go into bankruptcy. He got on the morning train headed for the factory. The manager offered him fifty rocking horses for his shares. After looking at their books, Sam considered himself lucky to get the rocking horses. He brought them back with him and sold them one by one over the years as children's Christmas presents. But there were still quite a few of them left when the Ellsworth Hotel burned to the ground, the rocking horses with it. Sam never got his money back.

Instead of rebuilding, Sam bought the Lonesome Pond property still farther back in the woods where the road to Inlet leaves the state highway. He didn't like the name and changed it to Sunny Pond, as it is known to this day. Here he operated a small hotel and carried on his work of bringing civilization into the woods. He never allowed any women in the bar unless accompanied by male escorts and rented no rooms to couples he suspected were not married.

Maybe Sam's greatest contribution was the whiskey he made during

SAM SPAIN
Sam's favorite recreation was horseback riding during the years he ran the Ellsworth Hotel.
(*Courtesy Carrie Spain*)

prohibition. He knew good whiskey himself, and his standards were high. People from downstate cities used to enjoy his product. Once a party from Syracuse tried to play a joke on him. Convinced that his whiskey was just as good as a famous Canadian brand and that no one could tell the difference, they had a bartender in Montreal pour some of Sam's whiskey into an empty bottle labeled with the name of the Canadian brand. On their way home to Syracuse they stopped off at Sam's and presented him with the bottle. Glowing with satisfaction at the brand name, Sam opened the bottle and poured a drink for himself and each of the Syracusans. His face changed expression immediately. "Why, you SOB's," he said, "that is my own whiskey."

Nearly all visitors from the outside liked Wanakena and the Cranberry region in general in late spring, summer, and fall. But most of them wanted nothing to do with our winters. They would hear about temperatures down to forty or forty-five degrees below zero. In recent years a weather station on top of Whiteface Mountain, which is over three thousand feet higher than Wanakena, has usually nosed us out as the coldest spot in the state, but for many years Wanakena was often the station reporting the lowest temperature. In January and February my ham radio friends would always ask me to read the thermometer outdoors. When I did, the sound waves got bumpier with their sympathetic shivers. It made no difference to tell them that ours is a dry cold and really very comfortable and invigorating once you get used to it.

"What do you do up there in winter?" the hams used to ask me before we got the snowmobile. Only rarely would they come up and see for themselves.

One cold winter day many years ago I was talking with a ham from Rochester over my shortwave station. He wanted to know about the road conditions from Star Lake to Saranac Lake. I told him the roads were plowed out and in good driving condition. He said that he and his family were driving to Saranac.

The following Saturday afternoon a car stopped outside my house, and the Rochester man, his wife, and two teen-aged children got out and introduced themselves. They were on their way home. They brought in the largest picnic basket I ever saw, loaded with food we could not get up in this country. The evening meal looked like a banquet. During the table conversation the wife asked what we did on a Saturday night to break the monotony of looking at trees and snow. She said they generally went to a nightclub, but she supposed we didn't have any nightclubs up here in the wilderness. I spoke right up, "That's

SAM SPAIN'S CAMP AT SUNNY POND

Sam (at right), his chef (in apron), and guests on the porch of the small hotel he operated after the Ellsworth burned.

(*Courtesy Carrie Spain*)

what you think. I will take you to a nightclub such as you have never seen and guarantee you will have more fun than you ever did in any Rochester club." She was all excited, and after the dishes were put away and the children given a telephone number to call in case of emergency, we took off for Benson Mines.

The place we went to was a restaurant and beer parlor that had outlasted all its competition in Benson Mines. Mrs. Clara Trombley, the proprietress, was a popular hostess known from the North Woods to Syracuse for her special weekend suppers and the congenial atmosphere of her place. The main room had a bar across one side, booths on the other, and a stage at the far end for the band. I won't call them an orchestra, for they made more noise than any orchestra that ever tuned up.

When we arrived we noticed a sign on the entrance door that read, "No neckties allowed." There were several empty booths, the band instruments were on the stage, and the players were at the bar getting tuned up. Soon the Saturday night couples began to arrive. It was an unwritten rule of the place that you were not one of the gang if you

SAM'S OTHER GUESTS
Sam Spain fed the deer all winter at his Sunny Pond camp.

(*Courtesy Carrie Spain*)

danced with your wife. Most couples were wearing red and black, gray and black, and other color combinations of lumberjack shirts sticking out of their pants. Most of the men had high-top boots. The girls had every type of footwear except shoes with open toes. They knew they would get stepped on as the evening advanced and the floor got more crowded.

Soon a young girl with a bundle in her arms asked my friend's wife if she would mind taking care of the baby. Determined to be a good sport, the Rochester woman said, "Sure, I'll be glad to." At the end of the bench there was room to lay the infant down. It opened its eyes only once and gave its new temporary mother a smile.

A hardy looking, partly inebriated friend of mine, a lumberjack but always a gentleman, came over to our booth, bowed very low, and said, "Mr. Keith, do you think your lady friend would dance with me?" Before I could catch my breath, she said, "Certainly." The few high-balls she had had must have been working. This Romeo had high-top lumberjack boots with laces dragging on the floor. He had a reputation for excelling in three activities—dancing, drinking, and working in the woods. This night he had the characteristic smell of the lumberjack,

143

which is hard to get rid of on weekends much before Sunday night. It was amazing to see the artistic dancing of this couple. Every other couple kept in the clear when the laces dragged by. After a while he returned his partner to our table and graciously thanked her. Later she told us she had never danced with such a good partner and had got a big kick out of it. As the evening wore on, she had more dancing partners, but when it came time for the closing dance, she was again with the lumberjack.

Several amusing things happened during the course of the evening. Someone kept changing the "Gents" and "Ladies" signs, and this led to a lot of confusion. A girl from Vrooman Ridge passed out from too many of her friends' buying her drinks. A couple of fellows carried her out and put her in her husband's car. Since it was a bitter cold night, they started the motor with the key they found in the ignition. (No one in those days ever locked car or house.) After a while her husband started looking for her. He had been busy all evening with a little French-Canadian girl who was visiting her aunt at Benson Mines. When he heard what had happened, he said, "My gal, she must be asphyxiated by now. My muffler has a bad hole in it and the fumes come right inside the car." He was afraid to go and look at her, so another boy volunteered. When the car door was opened and the motor shut off, the girl was found unconscious. Everyone thought she was dead. The local doctor was called. He came over in a few minutes and examined the girl. Then he bawled out the husband for calling him over just to see a woman dead drunk. His fee was three dollars, but he got a tip from the boys that cheered him up enough so that he joined them in a drink to celebrate the close call.

Things returned to normal after the doctor left. The young man took his wife home, and I heard later that she did not come to until noon the next day, missing church. She had to wait another day before telling her friends what a swell time she'd had at the dance.

As the night wore on, the talking and laughing got louder and louder. The band boys worked hard to make the music overcome the noise. The bass drum could be heard all the way to Star Lake. The ham and fish supper Mrs. Trombley served at midnight was something my friends said they would never forget. How could the cook make things taste so much better than at home? "It must be the Adirondack air," I said.

We were about to leave when the baby made a little sigh. My friend had forgotten all about it. Soon after, a young man came rushing in and asked if anybody had his baby. My friend spoke up, "Is this one yours?" Taking it, he said, "We got halfway home and I asked my wife where the baby was. She said, 'I think I left him in the dance hall.'" He was really mad. Though he hadn't paid a bit of attention to his wife all evening, he blamed her for everything.

My friend asked about the baby's sleeping all evening amidst the noise of the band and dancers. I told her, stretching the truth a little, that we used baby sitter's pills in this section. She thought that was awful. "It sure is," I said.

The next morning before my friends left, the wife said, "You certainly have something we don't have in Rochester," and thanked us for a fine evening. I haven't mentioned what my ham friend was doing all evening, for I don't think his wife would like the company he was with.

That once popular place has now been converted to an American Legion clubhouse. But I'll always remember it as the liveliest nightclub in the North Woods, where the guests could be counted on to supply the floor show.

20. WILFRED'S TRIAL

The saddest days of a guide's life are probably those when the realization grows on him that he is too old for active guiding. This time of life was especially hard for Wilfred because his love for the woods was the center of his being. Even after he gave up regular guiding, he spent much time upriver, going about to his friends' camps, helping to entertain their guests, and helping with camp chores. Often he wandered off alone into the woods.

About five years before his death Wilfred had one triumph that helped to shore up his spirits in old age. It started with his arrest, one day in 1933, by a game protector named Cone at Art Leary's camp near Round Hill Rapids. The charge was illegal possession of venison. The trial was held in the Oswegatchie Town Hall on December 19 of the same year, with Judge Otto Hamele presiding. A game protector by the name of Homer Duffy acted as attorney for Protector Cone. The defendant, Wilfred Morrison, was without counsel, for his attorney was sick. The trial had been adjourned once, and Judge Hamele refused to adjourn it again.

Wilfred's friends were in the courtroom. None of us will ever forget the occasion, though we have grown hazy about the details with the passage of years. One of us, however, had presence of mind enough to keep a record. She could tell from Wilfred's sprightly manner, as he surveyed the sympathetic faces of his friends, that the trial was likely to be interesting. She didn't have any notepaper with her, but she did have a pencil and a batch of Christmas cards. She scribbled notes on the blank spaces of the Christmas cards and later made a typed version. The following account is closely based on this unofficial record made by Mrs. Laura Ward, formerly of Wanakena, now of Saranac Lake.[22]

Court convened at 1:35 p.m. Duffy read the violation and stated the case against Wilfred. Then Protector Cone was called to the stand and asked by Duffy in what capacity he served as a witness. Cone replied that he was a game protector for the State of New York and had been one since March, 1931. Then he was asked what he had done on December 5, 1933. Cone replied that he had been notified by the home office in Watertown that he would be picked up in Harrisville. He went on to say that he had left Wanakena early in the morning with game protectors Duffy and Bush and a state trooper and had walked across the Plains to High Falls, where Duffy had told him to go to a camp over near the river. He and Bush had searched this camp and found everything all right there. Then they had walked along the river and taken a canoe that was at Round Hill Rapids to cross the river to another camp.

Wilfred had already interrupted the testimony once or twice and had been silenced by Judge Hamele. Now he interrupted again, "Do you tink I would leave de canoe handy for you if I had been breaking de law?" "Wilfred," Judge Hamele said sternly, "you'll have to be quiet. You'll have your turn to talk. *Now keep still.*"

CONE: As I was saying, we took this canoe and crossed the river and went over to this other camp—I think it is called the Leary Camp—and went in. Wilfred was in the first part—the cook tent, I guess, and . . . ("Dat is right," Wilfred interrupted; "I was preparing my lunch, and I ask dem to have a cup of coffee. I treat dem right." Judge Hamele rose to his feet, saying, "*Wilfred, you keep still.*") Well, yes, he was making coffee or something. I talked with him, then walked on alone through a partition into another room where the beds were and a stove, and then

146

came back in the front part of the tent. There was a big box with bacon, bread, etc. I looked through that. Wilfred opened it so we could see . . . ("Yes, I treat dem like gentlemen," Wilfred interrupted.) It was full of provisions. It was at the end of a long table. All the time Wilfred kept backing toward the other end of the table where the pack basket was . . . ("Whoa boy," Wilfred muttered, "be careful dere what you say.") Well, I don't know whether he did it on purpose or not, but it seemed so to me, as if he was trying to hide the basket. ("My lan," Wilfred interrupted again, "I did not know dere was anyting to hide.") I pulled out the basket and found two pieces of meat.

At this point Protector Duffy arose and unwrapped the meat, naming it Exhibit A. It was in a shallow cake tin, about ten inches long and seven inches wide. As he placed it on the corner of the table in front of the jury, Wilfred slid out of his chair and slowly walked to the box-stove to flick the ashes from his cigarette, muttering as he went, "My lan, I would not be guilty of dirtying a pot wid dat."

DUFFY: Is this the same meat you took out of that basket?

CONE: Yes, for it has been right in my possession ever since.

DUFFY: Go on.

CONE: I found these two pieces of venison . . . ("Be careful, boy," Wilfred said; "you have not prove it is venison." Hamele quieted him again.) . . . in that pack basket and it was fresh. It wasn't frozen, nor had it been frozen, for when I picked it out of the basket, I got blood on my hands. When we got to Wanakena, there was still blood on my fingernails, and it wouldn't rub off when I wiped it with a handkerchief. Wilfred claimed he didn't know anything about it, but as he was the only man in camp, I took him along. I told him he would have to go along with me as he was without a license or a permit to keep venison. We waited until he dumped out some water that was in a pan on the stove. (Wilfred whispered aloud, "Yes, dat is right—de reason, dat it would freeze and spoil de pot.") Wilfred was ahead on the trail, and he had on this coat and this pair of pants. (Protector Cone picked them up from the table and started handling them—Exhibit B—to show the jury the spots.) There was a drop of blood on that wool, and it was fresh in one lump—it was fresh all right because it hadn't had time to soak in. (Wilfred almost rose from his seat, saying, "Be careful dere, you are on de stand, you better not swear to a lie. Blood, my lan, I was . . ." Duffy interrupted, "*Wilfred, you keep still.*") And there were streaks of blood on these pants. (He had some difficulty in locating the streaks.) You could see where the blood had run down from his pants onto his boots.

147

And that blood was fresh—it wasn't dark. I took this coat and pants as evidence. We crossed the river, and when we got to the trail, Protector Duffy was there.

DUFFY: Did you notice any blood on the defendant's hands? (Before Cone had a chance to answer, Wilfred said, "My lan, blood, dere was no blood on my . . ." Hamele and Duffy both silenced him.)

CONE: Not until Protector Bush called my attention to it at Five Ponds Trail. Protector Bush first noticed the blood on his hands.

DUFFY: Are you sure it was blood?

CONE: Yes, there's nothing in the woods at this time of year to make stains like that. ("You do not know what you say!" Wilfred shouted. "I had to break de branch in de trail all de way to camp—dey were covered wid ice and hanging in de path. My lan, you should know . . ." Duffy silenced Wilfred.)

DUFFY: Was there any other party near or around this camp?

CONE: No, I didn't see anybody, and Wilfred told me he was alone. ("Yes, now you tell de trut," said Wilfred.)

Protector Bush was next called to the stand, and Duffy gave Wilfred instructions not to talk any more until it was his turn. In reply to Duffy's questions, Bush said that he had served the State of New York as game protector for two years, and that on December 5 he had accompanied Protector Cone to the camp where they had found Wilfred, as already related.

BUSH: We talked with Wilfred, and I searched around boxes and stuff that were in the cook tent and then looked around the beds and under the beds in the other part. Then I came back out and was standing by the front door when I noticed Protector Cone pick these two pieces of meat out of a pack basket. (Wilfred said in an undertone, "Now he call it *meat*.")

DUFFY: Are you sure these are the same two pieces?

BUSH: The meat exhibited is the same meat. Then I accompanied Protector Cone and Wilfred to the river.

DUFFY: Did you notice any blood on the defendant's coat and breeches?

BUSH: Yes, sir.

DUFFY: And did you notice any blood on the defendant's hands?

BUSH: Yes, sir. (Wilfred started protesting again, "Whoa boy, you had better not lie on de stan. My lan, didn't dey try to make me say it was blood, too? It was not, I tell you, and I would tell de trut. De reason, it will do you no good to tell a lie.")

148

DUFFY: And was this at the camp?

BUSH: Yes, just as we went out the camp door.

DUFFY: Are you positive it was blood?

BUSH: Yes, sir, because when we got to Wanakena, there were flakes of it around his fingernails and it was a stain that wouldn't come from any vegetation. (Wilfred couldn't contain himself. "My lan, didn't dey get me in de post office corner and try to make me say it was blood, de two of dem? I told dem I was not crazy—it was stain from breaking de brush on my way on de trail, and dey know dat!")

DUFFY: Did you have any conversation as to whether there was anybody else around the camp?

BUSH: No, sir.

Protector Bush was excused and Wilfred called to the stand.

DUFFY: Wilfred, tell us what you did on December 5, 1933.

WILFRED: My memory is not as good as yours. De reason, you are better educated, but I will tell de trut . . .

DUFFY: Come on, Wilfred, just tell us what you did on December 5.

WILFRED: I had been at de camp about twenty minutes and was going to make myself a little coffee and was placing de coffee can back in de cupboard—it was right near de door—and I saw dem coming. Dey were about twelve rod from de camp. I knew dey were game warden by de legging, and dey were hustling to get dere, too. When I saw dem, I said to myself, "Tank God, dey have noting on me." I had left Wanakena about 9:30 in de morning, and when I got to camp, I set de clock for 3:30—I had no watch, so I could not tell for sure de time. And I use dem right. I offered dem a cup of coffee, and I opened up de bread box for dem to see. Dey looked all around. Dey left everyting in perfect condition, just as dey found it. Dey didn't ask me if it was my basket nor anyting else, but dey found someting in de pack basket. I didn't know it was dere, not until dey pick it out. Anybody can get into de camp. We can't lock it—de reason, dat it is on state land.

At this point Judge Hamele asked Wilfred to wait a minute. He and Duffy were making notes of the testimony. While they were busily engaged writing, Wilfred slipped out of his chair and eased out of the room. When Judge Hamele looked up to ask him to continue, the witness chair was empty.

JUDGE HAMELE: Well, where's the defendant?

Someone near the door opened it, walked out into the corridor, and brought Wilfred back. He entered very nonchalantly and took his seat across the table from Protector Duffy and Judge Hamele. Had he asked

149

for permission to leave the room, someone no doubt would have accompanied him, and Wilfred was well aware of this. His was a very special mission, for somewhere on his person, we found out later, he had a bottle of Spain's Pride. Just at that moment he had felt the need of some. It seemed to give him renewed courage to continue.

JUDGE HAMELE: Wilfred, didn't you know that meat was there?

WILFRED: I knew de pack basket was dere—two of dem—but I didn't know de meat was dere. My lan, if I knew *dat*, I wouldn't leave it in plain sight when I hear dem coming.

DUFFY: So you heard them coming, Wilfred? Were they making any noise?

WILFRED: Noise? My lan, dey were coming like two bull trough de brush fence!

DUFFY: What time did you say you left Wanakena, Wilfred?

WILFRED: I had no watch, but I should say about 9:30—it was after you had cross de bridge.

DUFFY: Did you see anybody on your trip?

WILFRED: Yes, I met Andy near de Dobson Trail.

DUFFY: Wilfred, how far is it from Wanakena to camp?

WILFRED, after a few seconds' pause: Well, I would say about five mile, but you can find out for sure. It was measure just a few day ago by some state men.

DUFFY: And you mean to say that it took you from 9:30 until 3:30 to walk to camp?

WILFRED, very excitedly—Spain's Pride was taking effect: My lan, de trail was icy. You know dat. De branch all hanging down. Sometime you could not tell de trail. De boat was gone when I reach de river. I had to wait about two hour. Besaw or his partner—I can't tell dem apart—had de canoe. I didn't know why and I didn't ask dem. De reason, dat I never ask any question about ting that are none of my affair. When dey brought it back, I cross de river and he help me chop ice in de bay. De reason, dat when Art come, he can land de boat on de south side of de river. I was not hunting. I went up to get some boat at High Fall to bring to de camp, to earn a few dollar. I have witness to say I had no gun. My lan, you can kill a dog wid a club, but you can't kill a deer.

DUFFY: You just said you chopped ice from the river. Then how could you bring a boat down the river?

WILFRED: My lan, I was going to High Fall from Art's camp to see if I could. It had been thawing and sleeting. De river was not froze in de rapid. I was chopping ice in de bay so Art would have a place to land de canoe next day. And dey hear me chopping. Dat is why dey come across.

Wilfred was excused and Protector Cone called back to the stand.

DUFFY: Wilfred, if you have any questions to ask Protector Cone, you may ask them now.

WILFRED: No, I have told what dere is to tell. What difference would it make, when dey do not tell de trut? I would tell de trut if I was in dair place, and . . .

DUFFY: Wilfred, I said you could ask a question if you wanted to. Now have you any to ask?

WILFRED, smoking a cigarette and looking out the window in a meditative mood, then suddenly looking directly at Protector Cone: Did you ask me if that was my basket?

CONE: No.

WILFRED: Dat is all.

Protector Cone was excused from the stand. Protector Duffy now read the pertinent section of the New York State game law to the jury and restated the charge against the defendant: illegal possession of venison. He said he trusted the jury would do their duty and that from the evidence given, the defendant was apparently guilty of this violation.

FOREMAN OF THE JURY, addressing the judge: Your honor, are we to assume that Exhibit A is venison? To my knowledge, it has not been proved. And about the basket—nobody asked if it was his and it looks as if anybody could get into this camp.

WILFRED, in an undertone: My lan, it would take a chemist six month to prove dat it was venison, and dere has not been time.

DUFFY, annoyed, addressing the jury: You men have listened to this evidence, haven't you? And you have heard the charge against the defendant. Must I read this over again to you?

MR. NORTON, a man near the door, rising: Your honor, I have a message from a party in behalf of the defendant. He knows that Wilfred didn't have . . . (Here Judge Hamele ordered the speaker to keep still and sit down.)

NORTON: Well, I just wanted to say . . .

JUDGE HAMELE: Sit down, I tell you.

Mr. Norton sat down. Then Protector Duffy told Wilfred he could state his case to the jury. Wilfred arose from his chair and walked slowly to the other end of the table facing the jury.

WILFRED: Gentlemen, I do not know you and you do not know me. I went to Art's camp to earn a few honest dollar. Anybody can use de

151

camp. De reason, we can't lock it on state land. Some come and leave provision. Other come and clean house. I have witness here who know I did not have a gun. My hand were dirty and stained from chopping de ice and cleaning out de trail. It was not blood, and dey could not make me say it was. My lan, dey took my coat and pant and I could not work at de school. He did not ask me if dat was my pack basket. Now, gentlemen, whichever way you decide, dere will be no hard feeling from me to you or from you to me. Gentlemen, do your duty.

Contrary to usual proceedings, the spectators were asked to leave the room while the jury arrived at a verdict. They didn't have long to wait in the cold corridor and the adjoining unheated room. In less than five minutes the jury arrived at its verdict—not guilty.

In spite of the fact that the defendant was acquitted, Protector Cone insisted on keeping Wilfred's coat and breeches, saying that he was sending them to Albany and he'd get a conviction in the case or know why. Through the efforts of Wilfred's friends, however, his clothing was returned from Harrisville on January 14, 1934. The case was tried again at Canton, the county seat, and again the defendant was acquitted.

Mrs. Ward, the supplier of these notes on Wilfred's trial, wants me to add that her record is not complete. There are gaps here and there where laughter in the courtroom prevented her from hearing some of the testimony.

Wilfred became a popular hero in Wanakena after his acquittal, but old age soon began nibbling away at his satisfaction over his new renown. The alertness he had shown at the trial began to desert him. He became a little mixed up in his mind. He could still walk long distances, though, and continued to find excuses for going into the woods.

One cold morning in late March, two or three years after the trial, the crust was solid enough to walk on. The sun was under the clouds, and it seemed unlikely that a thaw would soften the three feet of snow during the day. Wilfred came to my house and said, "I will walk over to your camp and brush de snow off de roof. Then I'll go over to Art's and clean his roof." This would make about a twelve-mile trip.

When the afternoon turned toward darkness and Wilfred had not returned, I began to worry about him. He had agreed to let me know when he got back. So I walked up the grade and in about a quarter of a mile met Wilfred. "What took you so long?" I asked. "I saw five deer at Big Shallow Pond," he replied. I asked what he was doing at Big Shallow, three miles beyond Art's camp. He grinned and said, "I took de wrong trail when I left Art's, and when I saw de pond, I knew I had gone de wrong way." The side trip had added six miles to the twelve.

In the following summer Wilfred made his last long trip into the woods. Art and I were walking to Art's camp and Wilfred was behind us. His pace had slackened. This was the first time we had noticed it. When we got to the spot where the trail turned down a little incline to the site of the Carlson switch on the old logging railroad, we could not see Wilfred. We went back a way and hollered for him. His faint reply came from almost the top of Little Roundtop Mountain. "What are you doing up there?" we asked. "I am cleaning up de trail," came the reply. But there was no trail in that place. When he came down, we did not say a word about his being lost. We sensed that this was the end of one man's companionship with the woods.

21. THE OSWEGATCHIE YEARS LATER

A few years ago I became acquainted with Wesley Hammond of Leicester, New York, through shortwave radio transmission, both of us being amateur radio operators. Wes had heard so much about the Oswegatchie River that he wanted to make a canoe trip on it from Inlet to the headwaters. I wanted to go too. It had been twenty years since I had gone the full thirty miles to the headwaters.

We made the trip in the month of September, after the Labor Day exodus and before the hunting season. The river was fairly high from recent rains. Since I wasn't up to paddling so great a distance anymore, we had a two-horsepower outboard on our fifteen-foot aluminum canoe. This way of traveling was only slightly faster than paddling but was much easier and left Wes free to use his camera. He had also brought a tape recorder. He took color slides of many places on the river. Sitting in the bow, I recorded on tape what I had to say about campsites, feeder streams, spring holes, rapids, and other features of the winding river. I explained how places got their names and told about the river guides I had known since my first coming to Wanakena in 1907 and about still earlier ones I knew only from hearsay.

THE OSWEGATCHIE TODAY—FOOTBRIDGE AT INLET

Swinging from suspension cables, the log bridge spans the river where the Albany Trail used to cross.

(*Courtesy Stephen S. Slaughter*)

It was a good trip. Thanks to the off-season month, we didn't see any campers. The river seemed deserted. On our way back downstream, we stopped at Camp Johnny under Pine Ridge. Here on the little elevated clearing at a bend in the river we set up a light tent, had a fine steak supper, and slept well after getting some quarrelsome coons quieted down.

It was a good trip, but I missed the old guide camps and the cheerful greetings that used to come from them. All are gone now. Instead, the State Conservation Department has built lean-tos at Griffin Rapids and High Falls. These shelters are often dirty, and firewood around them is scarce from overuse. On our way below High Falls I wanted Wes to see the site of the old guide camp I shared with Clarence till we tore it down a quarter century earlier. Alders had completely covered over the landing. We had to claw our way through them, and then I could hardly recognize the campsite. Trees eight inches in diameter were now growing in the yard, and the little meadow between the camp and the river was a thick alder bed. We found the corner of an old

154

bedspring sticking out of the ground where the fruit cellar had been and where we had buried it in dismantling the camp.

As we continued our journey downstream, the nice weather left us and it began to rain. We arrived at Inlet wet and hungry. The state had recently purchased the land where Inlet House had stood. Now there is no place to get a hot meal or a cup of coffee when one comes out of the woods. Nor is there a place to rent boats and get supplies.

It seems to me now, as I look back over the changes of my lifetime, that even the few good things that have happened to the river have their bad sides. When the state bought the lands of the old Rich Lumber Company and added them to the forest preserve, logging was permanently stopped on the river above Wanakena. And the woods have made a good recovery in the sixty years they have been left alone. But regulations of the State Conservation Department have put an end to the life of the guide camps. And, if there are no more logging trains chugging, clanking, and belching smoke up to Dead Creek Flow and the Plains, another evil has taken their place—the noise and fumes of the outboards on the river. Not to speak of the jet planes overhead.

THE OSWEGATCHIE TODAY—A BEND
Motorboats also ply the narrow river, and leave oil slicks.

(Courtesy Dwight Church)

The Oswegatchie was a beautiful wild river when the white man took it from the Indians. Throughout its course from the ponds and springs of the Adirondack highlands to its mouth in the St. Lawrence River, it was lined with noble trees which turned it into a canyon of green boughs. Its waters were clear, free flowing, and alive with fish and game.

The last hundred and fifty years have brought more changes in the river than the preceding thousands. First, the forests of the lowlands in the St. Lawrence Valley were stripped. Then dams were built. And with the growth of population and industry, pollution crept upward from the mouth of the river, reaching to within a few miles of the Cranberry Lake outlet by 1900.

In the upper Oswegatchie all of the drastic changes have taken place since 1900, in a mere seventy years. The few sportsmen, trappers, and guides who knew the river above Wanakena before that date disturbed it hardly more than the Indians had done. Even after the turn of the century, the guides I knew in early and middle life were natural conservationists. They took no more fish and game than they could eat and tried to teach their parties to do likewise. The first major change in the upper river came with the logging operations of the Rich Lumber Company. The second, a more lasting and devastating assault on the river, was the coming of the modern sport in automobile and outboard motor.

The upper river is still relatively unpolluted. Except for the spewings of outboards, it still has the honest color of an unspoiled Adirondack stream, the color of weak coffee, a transparent tannin stain from the duff of evergreen forests. But the stream that once danced with jumping trout of all sizes is now still. The large trout have all been fished out, and the river today is nearly lifeless. As I came down it with Wes, it seemed as though even the good old smell of the woods had gone from its riffles and rapids.

The new generation of campers knows nothing of the character and woods skill required of the old-time guides and misses the tales of interest told by them which they gathered over the years. How bad Wilfred Morrison and the other guides of his generation would feel if they could see, hear, and smell what a mess the automobiles, planes, and outboard motors have made of our forests.

In setting down this book, I have tried to describe my experiences just as I lived them and to show how the great green forest and the old guides, who made the woods their home and life's work, appeared to me.

156

NOTES

1. The Rich Lumber Company made two land purchases in Township 15 (Emilyville) late in the year 1901. On October 15, Marquis L. Keyes and Helen P. Keyes of Oneonta, New York, sold the northeast quarter of the township (7,289 acres, with a few small exclusions) to Horace C. Rich of Buffalo and Herbert C. Rich of Cattaraugus, New York, for $115,000. On November 1, George F. Underwood and his wife of Fort Edwards, New York, and Frank L. Bell and his wife of Glens Falls, New York, sold the southeast quarter of the same township, 8,266 acres, to Horace and Herbert Rich for $115,000. The latter purchase was bounded on the west by a tract of state forest preserve and on the east by lands of another lumber company.

2. Cranberry Lake is the largest body of water in the Adirondack Forest Preserve and, since the flooding of the Sacandaga Reservoir and the inclusion of Lake George within the Blue Line, the third largest in the Adirondack Park. The firmly established local tradition is that there are 160 or 165 miles of shoreline. The estimate in the state recreation circular, "Trails in the Cranberry Lake Region," on the contrary, is 55 miles. The latter appears to be a point-to-point measurement, ignoring the indentations of a very irregular shore and the islands. Anyone who thinks the local estimate too high gets little support from Cranberry Lakers. "Just you measure it," they say.

3. The Rich Lumber Company prohibited the sale of intoxicating liquor on their lands in Township 15. When in 1913 the company sold most of its holdings in the township to Walton F. Andrews of Wanakena, Clayton R. Rich of Cattaraugus, and Leonard G. Willson of Wanakena, the deed carried the provision: "The party of the second part and their heirs shall not at any time manufacture or sell, as beverage, any intoxicating liquor nor permit the same to be done on the premises hereby conveyed, unless the Rich Lumber Company, its successors or assigns, shall sell other lands at the village of Wanakena without similar restriction or shall manufacture or sell such liquor at said village or permit the same to be done on any other land now owned by the company." On January 13, 1919, however, the Rich Lumber Company released the three above-named purchasers from the restrictions on liquor. The reprieve was short-lived. In the summer of the same year the prohibition law became effective for the whole country. It is questionable that any serious deprivation ensued under either local regulation or federal law.

4. There is evidence that the first white man of record to travel from the Mohawk Valley to the Upper St. Lawrence River reached the Oswegatchie River, two days' journey from its mouth, by an Indian trail which followed the general route of the Albany Trail. The year was 1653, when Joseph Antoine

157

Poncet, a French Jesuit priest and missionary, was escorted back to Canada by an Indian guard after being held prisoner by the Mohawks. See Paul F. Jamieson's "The First White Man Comes to St. Lawrence County," *The Quarterly* (St. Lawrence County Historical Association), April 1968, pp. 3–4, 21–23.

5. About three miles above Inlet, the Oswegatchie enters a tract of about 4,500 acres which was part of the original forest preserve lands of 1885. Because of mostly swampy shores, however, few big trees are encountered till one reaches Griffin Rapids. Here, on rising banks west of the river, is an impressive forest of hardwoods and conifers which extends south to the county line. The river bends eastward above Griffin Rapids, however, and reenters second-growth timber for the rest of its course in St. Lawrence County.

6. The reference is to a 50,000-acre tract which may be the largest contiguous area of virgin forest left in the Northeast. Its survival was accidental and exceptional. Aside from the upper slopes of the higher mountains and a few remote isolated tracts elsewhere, all timberland within Adirondack Park boundaries has been lumbered at one time or another. Only a little over one hundred thousand acres of virgin forest remains. Nearly half of that total is in the single tract known as the Webb Purchase between the St. Lawrence County line and the Beaver River Reservoir or Stillwater, in northeastern Herkimer County and the northwestern corner of Hamilton County.

This tract was formerly owned by Dr. W. Seward Webb, builder of the Adirondack Division of the New York Central Railroad. In 1886 the state built a dam on the Beaver River at Stillwater to impound water and supply power to factories downstream on the Black River. The dam caused a backflow of twenty miles which flooded part of Dr. Webb's lands and allegedly prevented the harvest of timber on unflooded portions north of the new reservoir. Dr. Webb brought suit against the state for $184,350 in damages. Evidence at the trial in 1895 covers over fifteen hundred pages. It was alleged that the dam and reservoir interfered with the removal of timber in townships 37, 38, 42, and 43 of the Totten and Crossfield Purchase and in parts of townships 5 and 8 of John Brown's Tract, as well as flooding portions of these lands. The land north of the Beaver, which had never been lumbered, was now rendered useless for logging. Logs could not be floated on the river, the cheapest way. It was impractical to float them over the top of the dam. The reservoir itself was clogged with submerged timber and driftwood, and there was no current for floating anyway. Because of the drawing down of water in winter, the ice in the reservoir was too thin to support the hauling of logs over it. Moreover, the usable low land along the river was now flooded to the base of the hills in such a way as to make hauling by rail or road impossible on the north side of the reservoir. The mountain ranges there run nearly at right angles to the river, and loads of lumber or supplies could not be drawn across them. Agents for Dr. Webb maintained that, of the 120,000 acres of forest land he owned in the vicinity, 65,000 were completely cut off from lumbering by water, and 21,678 acres were completely cut off even for lumbering by rail, since logs could not be drawn over the mountains.

The claim for damages was finally settled by the state's agreeing to purchase 75,377 acres from Dr. Webb for $600,000. The Webb Purchase was completed in January of 1896, and the land so acquired became part of the state forest preserve, to be kept forever wild according to constitutional law. Of the 50,125 acres north of the Beaver River to the St. Lawrence County line, the 1896 report of the Commissioners of Fisheries, Game and Forests says: "They are covered with a primeval forest in which no lumbering operations or timber cutting whatever has been done, and on which no timber right has been granted or reserved. . . . No tourist or sportsman should claim a thorough knowledge of the Adirondack Wilderness until he has traversed the region included in this purchase." (*Second Annual Report of the Commissioners of Fisheries, Game and Forests, for 1896*, p. 459; for details of the trial and purchase, see pp. 376–460.)

The commissioners' self-congratulation seems ex post facto. The happy results stemmed more from chance than from intent. Dr. Webb had intended to harvest the timber on his land. In building the dam, the state had no thought of preventing him. The purchase was consummated primarily to settle a claim, not to acquire virgin timber. If only that sort of accident had happened oftener!

The Society of American Foresters has selected three specimen natural areas in the tract of the Webb Purchase, out of 128 such undisturbed areas in 34 states and Puerto Rico. These specimen areas, which range up to 150 acres in size, are called the Wolf Pond, the Five Ponds–Wolf Pond, and the Totten and Crossfield natural areas, designated for their stands of white pine, red spruce, yellow birch, beech, and sugar maple (see *Journal of Forestry*, November 1960, pp. 913–14).

7. There is no record of what caused the clearing known as the Plains. Some think it was caused by a windfall long ago. In that case, however, the rotting trees would have provided humus for a successor forest which should have developed long before now. Another possible explanation is a severe ground and crown fire that not only destroyed all the trees but bit so deeply into dry duff that it rendered the Plains infertile for a long period. A similar situation can be viewed today on barren land of a private preserve at Brandon, the result of a fire in 1903. Several attempts to get a new forest started there have failed, and only in recent years has scattered new growth appeared. The Plains of the Oswegatchie were in existence long before 1903, however. Young trees are now taking hold in some places.

8. Cornelius Carter (d. 1905) was a schoolmaster, lawyer, sportsman, guide, and poet. In his active career he served as deputy district attorney of St. Lawrence County. After becoming deaf, he settled alone in a log cabin on the Plains. There he took in guests and served as guide to sportsmen. One of his patrons was L. C. Smith, the typewriter manufacturer of Syracuse, who is said to have paid the costs of publishing a slender volume of Carter's poems. As a colorful character and one of the earliest guides of the region (he settled on the Plains in the late 1870s), Carter has had an important niche in local folklore. See David F. Lane's "Poet of the Adirondacks," *Ad-i-ron-dac*, November–December 1950, pp. 120–23; also Atwood Manley's *Rushton and His Times in American Canoeing* (Syracuse, 1968), pp. 5–7.

9. "Enacted here [at High Falls] each season is the thrilling drama of two

to four pound speckled trout vainly trying to leap the falls to do their spawning in the waters above, a spectacle not duplicated in the wild life world outside of Newfoundland and the Columbia River regions where salmon leap tumbling waters to get to their rearing beds. Because the big brook trout never make it at High Falls, only those of modest size are captured in the river above." (From David F. Lane's "Oswegatchie Country," *Ad-i-ron-dac*, July–August 1949, p. 77.)

10. All I have verified satisfactorily is that a film company did pass through Wanakena on its way to an encampment on Pine Ridge during the 1920s. A platform they built on the ridge remained for several years until it collapsed and rotted away, according to Fred Griffin, retired forest ranger of the town of Fine. David F. Lane identifies the film as a silent version of Cooper's *Last of the Mohicans*. An old hunter in the region identifies it as *Robin Hood*. Since the only versions of these two subjects made by American producers in the 1920s starred famous actors (Wallace Beery in both and Douglas Fairbanks, Sr., in the latter), both seem unlikely candidates. The *Watertown Daily Times* has no record of such a filming, and John B. Johnson, the editor and publisher, writes that the Adirondacks would never have recovered if Wallace Beery had been only seven miles from Wanakena making a motion picture. Fairbanks would have been a still more sensational presence.

It seems likely that less celebrated actors were involved. Two clues from old-timers who remember the picture as either "Daniel Boone" or "Chronicle of America" add up to a possibility. In the 1920s the Yale University Press produced a series of educational films entitled *Chronicles of America*, one of the series being *Daniel Boone*, released in 1923.

Today, the white pines of Pine Ridge are impressive for those viewing them for the first time; much less so to those who knew them before the hurricane of November 25, 1950, which felled over half the stand. The fallen giants were removed by salvage crews. Wilfred, of course, speaks of Pine Ridge as it was before the Big Blow. Today, the ten acre Wolf Pond Natural Area, designated by the Society of American Foresters, is a larger unmixed stand of white pines. Although the trees are not so old or tall as the biggest on Pine Ridge, they are rooted in deep glacial soil and are less stagnant.

The biggest single white pine in the Cranberry Lake region is across Inlet Flow from the Ranger School. It is sixty-two inches in diameter.

11. Wilfred refers to a successful attempt to restore beaver to the Adirondacks after they had been virtually exterminated for eighty years. In 1907 (the year of Herbert Keith's first visit to Wanakena and Wilfred's remark about the beaver) the man chiefly responsible for the restoration, Harry V. Radford, published an article entitled "History of the Adirondack Beaver" (*Annual Reports of the Forest, Fish and Game Commissioner of the State of New York for 1904–1905–1906*, Albany, 1907, pp. 389–418). The following details come from Radford's article.

In the Oswegatchie country the last large take of beaver skins—300—was in 1815, when a party of St. Regis Indians from Canada hunted there for a few weeks after the beaver had been left undisturbed for several years because of the War of 1812. After 1815 very few beaver were observed in the area. By

1820, Radford estimates, there were fewer than one thousand beaver in all the Adirondacks. They were never completely extinct, however. Low ebb was reached about 1895, when a small colony of five to ten continued to survive in a last refuge, the ponds and streams of Township 20 in Franklin County, northwest of Upper Saranac Lake.

Prompted by Radford and his association of sportsmen and naturalists, the State Legislature in 1904 gave the Forest Commission authority to purchase and liberate elk and beaver and made a small sum available for this purpose, with an additional appropriation in 1906. A few owners of private parks also cooperated. The effort to restore elk failed, but the restoration of beaver was a complete success. In the spring of 1905 Radford, assisted by the Brown's Tract Guides' Association, liberated six Canadian beavers on tributaries of the Moose River. By 1907 a total of thirty-four had been released and had already spread northward as far as the Beaver River. By the end of 1906, Radford estimates, there were seventy-five of the animals in the Adirondacks. Thereafter the number grew rapidly. Wilfred Morrison did not have long to wait to see beaver along the Oswegatchie.

12. The hunting season began on September 16, 1908, and brought hundreds into the dry woods. Fires started in many locations. The worst came in late September. After destroying Long Lake West (Sabattis), it swept over 30,000 acres of mostly cutover forest land as far as Cranberry Lake.

13. "Today, of all the vast primeval forest that encircled the lake in 1903, only one small tract remains and that because in the previous century it had become a part of the New York State Forest Preserve, to be forever kept, according to the State Constitution, as wild forest lands. This tract lies on either side of the Inlet, starting below the Ranger School, surrounding the Hawk's Nest, and extending south to Lansing's Point on Dead Creek Flow. To find a large tract of virgin timber in the Cranberry region today, one must go south of Five Ponds or High Falls." (From Fay Welch's "Making of a Woodsman," in *Cranberry Lake from Wilderness to Adirondack Park*, ed. Albert Vann Fowler, Syracuse, 1968, p. 201).

14. After pointing out that the New York State Ranger School is the oldest institution of its kind in North America and one of only two such schools in the United States, the school catalogue of 1966–1968 credits Hamele's initiative: "Founding of the school developed from an idea of J. Otto Hamele of Wanakena. He thought that nearby cutover lands considered useless might serve a useful purpose as an experimental area for the students and faculty of the new College of Forestry [in Syracuse]. Through Mr. Hamele's efforts, the Rich Lumber Company proposed that a research station be established at Wanakena."

Choosing to stay on in Wanakena, Hamele himself had some lean years after the closing of the mill. He ran the gasoline cars on the Cranberry Lake Railroad till the rails were torn up in 1917. In later years he clerked for a time in the general store, which was managed by his wife; he also ran a garage and did trucking. As justice of the peace, he served as judge in Wilfred Morrison's trial (see Chapter 20). He was supervisor of the town of Fine and in his last years historian of St. Lawrence County, the first to hold that office. Shortly before his death in 1947, he was engaged in founding the St. Lawrence County Historical Association.

15. Fide (Philo) Scott (d. 1911) stirred the folk imagination of the Cranberry Lake–Oswegatchie region more than any other of a dozen or more unique characters. As guide and friend of the once famous North Country novelist, Irving Bacheller, Scott even broke into literature. He is the subject of the ballad "Him an' Me" and of the profile "The Most Remarkable Character I Have Known" in *From Stores of Memory;* he is also the original of the hero in Bacheller's novel *Silas Strong: Emperor of the Woods* and provided traits for fictional characters in other novels and short stories. Some others who have written about Scott are: Albert Vann Fowler, in "The Hermit of Big Deer," *High Spots Yearbook,* 1940, and *Cranberry Lake 1845–1959,* ed. Albert Vann Fowler (Blue Mountain Lake, N.Y., 1959); David F. Lane, in "The Oswegatchie Country," *Ad-i-ron-dac,* July–August 1949; Paul F. Jamieson, in "The Oswegatchie Highlands," *Adirondac,* May–June 1963, and in "Guide and Party," *New York Folklore Quarterly,* June 1966. The following two stanzas are from a memorial poem "Lines on the Death of Filo Scott of Fine," written shortly after Scott's death by a near neighbor and friend, the Reverend C. Shaw:

> True friend of nature, nature's heart
> Entwined so close about his own
> He could not live from her apart,
> Each life had so together grown.
>
> .   .   .   .
>
> On tramp, in camp, on wave or shore,
> He was a wise and faithful guide.
> And we regret we'll see no more
> The genial face of Uncle Fide.

16. In 1919 the State Conservation Commission published the first list of registered guides, in accordance with an act of the legislature providing for registration. This practice has continued to the present.

The permits that Art Leary and other guides secured for camps on state land were issued under a system started in 1916. On the principle that temporary use of forest preserve land is all that can be allowed under the constitution, the Conservation Commission ruled that permits had to be secured by anyone wishing to set up a camp in a given locality for more than three nights. Regulations on the construction, materials, and conditions of tenure were also adopted.

17. George Muir is said to have killed "the last wolf" in the Cranberry Lake region in 1894, near his camp at Gull Lake (see Robert Marshall's "History of the Cranberry Lake Region," *Camp Log,* December 1922, p. 62). In October 1873, Verplanck Colvin, on reaching the "Lost Lake" (Big Deer Pond) he was looking for in the state surveys of that year, found a wolf trapper on its shores who turned out to be George Muir, accompanied by his brother John. George told Colvin of many lakes and ponds in the region that had not

162

appeared yet on any maps. Colvin proceeded to look for them. Muir Pond, north of Wolf Pond, is named for George.

18. Partly because of the remoteness of the area, the demand for guides in the Cranberry-Oswegatchie region held up a little longer than in other parts of the Adirondacks. It is interesting to compare Keith's reasons for the decline of guiding in the 1930s with a recent analysis of the obsolescence of mountain guides, in the high peak area, by the late 1920s. The following is from George Marshall's "Adirondack Guides of the High Peak Area," in *The Adirondack High Peaks and the Forty-Sixers*, ed. Grace L. Hudowalski (Albany, 1970), pp. 129–30:

1. Those who enjoyed climbing and could afford to employ guides became fewer.

2. The Conservation Department, and others, had marked and cleared main trails through the mountains.

3. Guides in some localities improved trails so they would not have to climb, thus promoting their own obsolescence.

4. The auto and improved roads enabled enthusiasts from central New York to drive to the Adirondacks for a weekend of climbing.

5. Lighter equipment and the improved physical condition of those who made wilderness climbs eliminated the "porter" function of guides.

6. The new competent self-help generation going into the mountains overnight could do their own camping.

7. Above all, a new generation of climbers learned to find its way among the mountains and to introduce its friends to them.

8. With the booming enthusiasm of growing numbers of Forty-Sixers in recent years, footpaths—or herd ways—have been formed on most of the trailless peaks, not only giving a final blow to guides, but also taking away much of the sense of adventure and pleasure of those who would like the challenge of finding their way up the High Peaks by their own woodcraft.

19. It is probably a mistake to attribute the decline of the Childwold Park House on Massawepie Lake to the coming of the railroad. On the contrary, the opening of the railroad in 1892 may have contributed to the popularity of the resort among the fashionable people who visited it in the 1890s, including British royalty and a United States President or two. It was built in 1889 by Addison Child, owner of the Childwold estate. Accommodating 300 guests in the main building and outlying cottages, it had a resident physician and operated its own farm. A piazza 400 feet long encircled the building. The lake, several ponds, and forest trails of a 16,000-acre park were at the disposal of guests. During the period of its greatest popularity, the resort was under the management of William F. Ingold, who also managed the Magnolia Springs Hotel in Florida.

The Childwold Park House was one of the earliest of the large Adirondack hotels to close, in the year 1907. Patronage fell off in the early years of the century after Addison Child's death and a change in management. The park is now owned by the Otetiana Council of the Boy Scouts of America, of Rochester and Monroe County, New York. It is an ideal playground for the scouts.

20. In the summer of 1970 an enlargement of the functions of the State Conservation Department took place, a new commissioner was appointed, and the name was changed to the New York State Department of Environmental Conservation. The new organization, like the old, has custody of the Adirondack Forest Preserve.

21. For a theory attributing the decline of brook trout, at least in part, to beaver dams in the Cranberry Lake region, see Charles Woolsey Cole's chapter, "The Passing of Brook Trout," in Albert Vann Fowler's *Cranberry Lake 1845–1959* (Blue Mountain Lake, N.Y., 1959), pp. 143–45. Mr. Cole points out the warming effect of beaver dams on the waters of streams. He also believes that trout of good size can not get through beaver dams or, by implication, jump over them.

22. Although a similar account of Wilfred's trial appeared in Albert Vann Fowler's *Cranberry Lake 1845–1959*, no apology is needed for this recast, the necessary climax of Wilfred's story.